STALIN

STALK

STALIN

A POCKET BIOGRAPHY

HAROLD SHUKMAN

In memory of
Dmitri Volkogonov

First published in 1999 by Sutton Publishing Ltd.
This paperback edition published in 2023

The History Press
97 St George's Place, Cheltenham,
Gloucestershire, GL50 3QB
www.thehistorypress.co.uk

British Library Cataloguing in Publication Data.
A catalogue record for this book is available from the British Library.

ISBN 978 1 80399 275 4

Typesetting and origination by The History Press
Printed and bound in Great Britain by TJ Books Limited, Padstow, Cornwall.

Trees for Life

Contents

Chronology

In February 1918 the Soviet government abolished use of the Julian (Old Style) calendar and adopted the Gregorian Western (New Style), which was thirteen days ahead (twelve days in the nineteenth century). Both dates are given here.

1878	**6/18 December**. Stalin born in Gori, Georgia
1879	**9/21 December**. Stalin's 'official' (incorrect) birthday
1888	Enters church school in Gori
1894	Admitted to Tiflis Seminary
1899	Expelled from Seminary
1902	**April**. Arrested
1903	**October**. Deported to Novaya Uda, eastern Siberia
	November. Escapes
1904	**January**. Adopts nickname Koba

June. Marries Yekaterina Svanidze

1905   **December**. Attends Bolshevik conference at Tammerfors, Finland, under pseudonym K. Ivanovich

1906   **March**. father dies in Tiflis

April. Attends Fourth Party Congress in Stockholm

1907   **September**. First son, Yakov, born

1907   **November**. Wife dies of tuberculosis or typhus Attends Fifth Party Congress in London Organizes bank robbery in Tiflis

1908   **March**. Arrested in Baku

1909   **February**. Exiled to Solvychegodsk, Northern Russia

June. Escapes

1910   **March**. Arrested

October. Sent back to Solvychegodsk Fathers a son by Maria Kuzakova

1911   Moves to Vologda under surveillance

August. Escapes to St Petersburg Re-arrested and sent back to Vologda

1912   **January**. Elected *in absentia* on to Bolshevik Central Committee

February. Escapes from Vologda

April. Re-arrested and deported to Narym, Western Siberia.

September. Escapes and returns to capital

November. Attends Bolshevik meeting in Cracow

1913   **January**. Visits Vienna, meets Trotsky and
         Bukharin
         Changes his name to Stalin
         February. Returns to St Petersburg as an
         editor of *Pravda*
         March. Arrested
         August. Exiled to Turukhansk on Arctic Circle
1917   **March**. Tsar Nicholas abdicates Stalin returns
         to capital, co-edits *Pravda* with Kamenev
1917   **August**. Delivers political report at Sixth
         Party Congress
         25 October/7 November. Bolshevik coup in
         Petrograd (St Petersburg)
1918–19 Serves as Military Commissar Southwestern
         Front
1918   Stalin and Nadezhda Alliluyeva register mar-
         riage **16 July**. Murder of Romanov family in
         Yekaterinburg
1921   Stalin's second son, Vasili, born
1922   **April**. Stalin becomes General Secretary of the
         Central Committee
1926   Stalin's daughter, Svetlana, born
1927   Kamenev, Zinoviev and Trotsky expelled
         from Central Committee
1929   **February**. Trotsky deported from USSR
         November. Bukharin expelled from Central
         Committee
1932   **8 November**. Stalin's second wife, Nadezhda
         Alliluyeva, commits suicide

1933	US recognizes USSR
	USSR enters League of Nations
1934	**February**. 'Congress of Victors'
	1 December. Kirov assassinated in Leningrad
1936	**August**. Zinoviev and Kamenev tried and shot
1937	**May**. Tukhachevsky and seven other marshals shot
1939	**August**. Nazi-Soviet Non-aggression Pact signed in Moscow
1940	**August**. Trotsky murdered in Mexico on Stalin's orders
1941	**22 June**. Germany invades USSR
1941	**July**. Stalin's son, Yakov, captured as POW
1942	Churchill in Moscow for talks with Stalin
1943	Stalin in talks with Churchill and Roosevelt in Tehran Stalin adopts rank of Marshal
1945	**February**. Stalin hosts Allied talks in Yalta Stalin adopts title of Generalissimo
	8 May. Victory in Europe Day in the West
	9 May. Soviet Victory Day
	July–August. Stalin attends Potsdam Conference
1952	**October**. Nineteent Party Congress
1953	**5 March**. Death of Stalin

1

Introduction

'I kiss you on the nose, Eskimo-fashion. Dammit! I miss you something awful. I miss you like hell, I swear. I have no one, not a soul to have a proper talk with, damn you. Is there really no way for you to come to Cracow?'[1] In December 1912, Stalin wrote to his party comrade Lev Kamenev, then in Geneva, in this jocular tone, very much as one Russian intellectual might write to another. Twenty-four years later, he would stage-manage Kamenev's trial as a 'Fascist spy' and have him shot like a dog.

In 1912, Stalin was regarded by his comrades as an audacious revolutionary and an affable comrade – indeed, Lenin described him as a 'wonderful Georgian'. By the 1930s, he had become a homicidal monster whose thirst for their blood seemed insatiable. When, in the late 1940s, for his own twisted purposes, he masterminded the arrest and in some cases the execution of the wives of some of his closest and longest-serving accomplices, the omnipotent dictator would sadistically respond to their pleas for mercy: 'It doesn't depend on me. I can do nothing. Only the NKVD [secret police] can sort it out.'[2]

What had wrought this transformation? How had a provincial, comparatively insignificant member of a small, unsuccessful group of journalists and persecuted political conspirators – which the Bolsheviks mostly were before the First World War – become one of the most powerful and merciless dictators in history, a dictator whose name and image would saturate every field of Soviet endeavour? How did that image evolve from the 'grey blur' depicted by one of the closest observers of 1917, and the 'outstanding mediocrity', as the revolution's most vivid personality called him, into a demigod, an icon worshipped by his own subjects, as well as by an international movement that included many educated and thoughtful people abroad?

Under Stalin's rule, what had been the Russian Empire was transformed no less spectacularly. When Lenin died in 1924 and Stalin took over the reins of power, the Soviet Union had barely begun to recover from the successive ravages of the First World War, the Civil War and the economic failures of the new regime. Both the industry and the agriculture of this predominantly agrarian country had been reduced to a shadow of their former scale. Yet by 1939 the Soviet Union was an industrial and military power of formidable strength. Driven in 1941 by Hitler's armies into its own heartland, by 1943 the Red Army turned the war around and by the spring of 1945 was sharing Europe with its Western Allies. Under Stalin's rule the USSR, a pre-war pariah among nations, took its place on the United Nations Security Council as the leader of the 'socialist camp' in a world that was soon to be divided by the Cold War.

As a member of the Politburo from 1917 and as its head from 1924, Stalin can be said to have been in power for thirty-six years, from the time of the revolution until his death in 1953. And since he left no personal diary – that we know of – the story of his life is inevitably and inextricably linked to the history of the period. It is the purpose of this brief account to examine these parallel transformations – Stalin's and the Soviet Union's – and to see how they are interrelated.

Beginnings

The Early Years

Stalin's birthday has always been given as 9/21 December 1879. The local archives now reveal that he was in fact born on 6/18 December 1878, a year earlier. There is no explanation for this discrepancy. His birthplace was Gori, a small town of some 12,000 inhabitants of mixed Caucasian origin, in the Georgian province of Tiflis (Tblisi), and close to the Borzhom source of mineral water that would remain Stalin's digestive of choice until the end of his life. Named Iosif (Joseph) and known by the Georgian diminutive of Soso, he was the third son of Vissarion (Beso) Dzhugashvili and Yekaterina (Keke), née Geladze. Two infant children had died before Soso arrived.

His father, Beso, was one of the small town's ninety-two cobblers, among the lowest ranking trades in the hierarchy of artisanry, the topmost being that of watchmaker. His brutishness, poverty and frustration made Beso a violent, drunken husband and father; his wife, a pious Christian, was a hard-working laundry-woman and seamstress. She was dedicated to her only child and determined that he should rise above his origins and, ideally, become a priest in the Orthodox Church. Violence and discord in the family home eventually led to the parents' separation and Beso ended up dying either in a Tiflis doss-house or after being knifed in a brawl. He was buried as a pauper.

A Georgian-speaker until the age of eleven – he would never lose the distinctive accent – thanks to his mother's efforts and the help of a sympathetic patron, Soso entered the church school in Gori in 1888. In 1894, having graduated with top marks, he was admitted to the Tiflis Seminary to train as a priest. Here he showed talent and a phenomenal memory for Biblical texts. Here also it was that, like so many other young people throughout the empire, he was swept up by the tide of discontent and rebellion that characterized Russia at the turn of the century. Peasants were rioting for more land; workers were striking for better conditions; students were demonstrating for their curricula to be liberalized; intellectuals were demanding political reform that would give society a voice in government; senior officials were being assassinated; anarchists were throwing bombs; Social Democrats were setting up clandestine organizations to bring the message of socialist revolution to the proletariat.

Soso and his fellow seminarists were ripe for conversion to the new political creed. The lack of intellectual stimulation in their studies and the drab harshness of seminary life made them vulnerable to the political ferment that was stirring in Russia, let alone the excitement of the colourful Georgian capital. While still playing the diligent theological student in class, Soso was reading Marx and Darwin. He became an atheist and began associating with underground, i.e. clandestine, revolutionary circles.

By 1899, the seminary and everything it stood for was insufferable to him. After ten years of religious education, at the age of twenty-one and no longer manageable in the seminary, he was expelled for indiscipline. As a fellow seminarist and revolutionary of the time wrote, the young Stalin took with him from the seminary 'a vicious, ferocious enmity against the school administration, against the bourgeoisie, against everything that existed in the country and embodied Tsarism. Hatred against all authority.'[1] Soso abandoned theology and entered the underground world of the Marxist organization in Tiflis where he became a professional revolutionary.

Revolutionary Youth

'Professional revolutionary': the term came into use around this time, as Vladimir Lenin was promulgating his ideas about the kind of revolutionary party he wanted to build, and the nature of the people he believed should constitute that party. They must be so dedicated to the cause that no personal or other goals would dilute their zeal or their submission to the 'Centre'. The Centre would be run by a small, self-appointed group of intellectuals who were themselves guided by the Leader, i.e. Lenin. 'The cause' was to overthrow tsarism and promote socialist revolution. Many of Lenin's recruits were qualified for a professional occupation – economist, physician, lawyer, scientist, some of them potentially distinguished – but most had either dropped out or been expelled from university or high school precisely because they had become actively involved in the revolutionary movement.

Apart from the priesthood, Soso was not a candidate for any other profession. Like many revolutionaries, his abilities as a political writer would find expression only in the party press: poems he wrote as a teenager offered little prospect of a successful literary career. But he was effective as a Marxist teacher of illiterate workers, his seminary education having provided him with an ability to convey complex ideas about the relationship between the economic and political system and the lives of ordinary people in a way they could understand. His simple style would become his hallmark, as both speaker and writer, in later life.

Along with the rewriting of history in general, Stalin's biography, especially the section covering the years leading up to and including the revolution of 1917, became an object of distortion and invention when he reached the pinnacle of power in the 1920s, and even more so in the 1930s when his status as Leader was elevated into near-deity. In all respects, his image was ruthlessly transformed. What is plain, however, is that in the early years of his revolutionary career in the Caucasus he was an audacious conspirator with a taste for the more nefarious and criminal aspects of revolutionary craft.

In April 1902 he was arrested in the Black Sea oil port of Batum and imprisoned. He was now a registered revolutionary with his mug shot and personal characteristics recorded by the local branch of the Okhrana, or secret police. No stranger to physical hardship and deprivation, he quickly adapted to prison life, but after eighteen months was deported to Novaya Uda, a village in the eastern Siberian province of Irkutsk. While he was there the Russian Social Democratic Party split, although it is unlikely that he heard about it until later.

For nearly three years, Lenin and his comrade, Yuli Martov, had worked from outside Russia to establish a network of committees inside the empire which would follow their ideological guidance. Their ideas were promulgated in a newspaper, called *Iskra* (*The Spark*), which was smuggled into Russia and distributed by agents. Gradually, by a mixture of persuasive argument, material inducement and even physical intimidation, *Iskra*'s agents gathered a substantial amount of support among local committees for their masters in Western Europe.

The First Congress of the Russian Social Democratic Workers' Party had taken place in Russia in March 1898, but within two weeks eight of the nine founding members had been arrested. By the summer of 1903, Lenin and Martov were ready to convene the Second Congress in Brussels and then London with more than fifty delegates from revolutionary bodies inside and outside Russia.

Their hopes for a united party, however, were dashed. First, a small number of significant organizations refused to accept *Iskra*'s leadership, and their recalcitrance caused cracks to appear elsewhere. Specifically, the Jewish Social Democrats, or Bund, claimed sole representation of Jewish workers in the party and this caused uproar among other delegates of Jewish origin – half of the entire attendance, according to Lenin's calculation. The Bund eventually left the Congress and the party when its demands were overwhelmingly rejected. (It was during these debates that Trotsky made his name, speaking up so frequently for Lenin's line that he was dubbed 'Lenin's cudgel', though he would soon move away and adopt an independent position.)

Secondly, Martov was affronted by the discovery that among *Iskra*'s delegates were a number who were obeying Lenin's orders blindly, as if he had created a separate following. Along this main fault line other issues, particularly affecting the personnel of the central bodies, e.g. the editorial board of *Iskra*, led to further differences. As a result of the disarray, the Congress split into two wings. Lenin led a temporary majority and called them Majorityites, or Bolsheviks, while Martov rallied the non-Leninist elements, dubbed by Lenin the Minorityites, or Mensheviks.

Many of the delegates and the leaders themselves were disappointed by their failure to create a united party. Inside Russia, activists and workers were disheartened by the split, finding the intellectuals' squabbles exasperating, and many continued to maintain non-sectarian, united organizations.

Winter in Siberia tested even the tough young Dzhugashvili's powers of endurance, and in January 1904 he escaped and made his way back to Tiflis. The Transcaucasian Social Democrats were already a mass movement, a feature they shared with other emerging socialist movements in the Russian borderlands, whether Polish, Ukrainian or Jewish, where the issue of social emancipation was linked to that of national liberation. Led by Noah Zhordania, the Caucasians resisted attempts to split their party into Bolsheviks and Mensheviks, and, at least until 1912, remained a unified movement of undifferentiated Social Democrats. Indeed, even the clandestine press in Baku, on which *Iskra* and dozens of other banned publications were produced in large print runs from 1901, was run jointly by Bolsheviks and Mensheviks without friction until 1905, when it became exclusively Bolshevik.

When Soso arrived in Tiflis he may already have been an admirer of Lenin. In any case, his role as a party worker in the Caucasus grew rapidly and acquired significance.

To evade police detection it was common for revolutionaries to adopt an alias: Lenin had been born Vladimir Ulyanov, Martov's real name was Julius Tsederbaum, and Trotsky had been Leon Bronstein, to name only three. In 1904 Iosif Dzhugashvili took his nickname from his favourite novel, *The Parricide* by Kazbegi, whose Robin Hood-like hero was called Koba, a name that would identify Soso until 1912, when he adopted the alias by which one day the world would know him.

Family

Lenin had married Nadezhda Krupskaya in a church ceremony only because her formidable mother would countenance nothing less. Consistent in their atheism, most revolutionary intellectuals preferred the more bohemian arrangements of common-law relationships in a country where civil marriage did not yet exist. Young women were drawn into the movement in large numbers, and with so many common cultural and political interests, to say nothing of the risks they shared, partnerships, some lasting, some ephemeral, were numerous, if not the norm.

This was less true in Georgia, where women lagged behind their Russian sisters in terms of feminine emancipation. Evidently Stalin was content with this aspect of his native culture, for in 1904, on his return to Tiflis, he married Yekaterina Svanidze, the sister of a fellow revolutionary, in a religious ceremony. Like Stalin's mother, she was a deeply pious peasant girl, a seamstress, and contentedly submissive to her husband. She created for him a haven of peace and stability to which he could escape from the hectic life he led as an underground organizer, on the rare occasions when he felt it was safe to do so.

Their son, Yakov, was born in 1907, but within a year Yekaterina had contracted tuberculosis or typhus and died. The cynical, hard-faced Koba was devastated. His friend, Soso Iremashvili, attended the funeral and recalled that Koba, pressing his hand and pointing to the coffin, said: 'Soso, this creature softened my stony heart. She is dead and with her have died my last warm feelings for all human beings.'[2] The baby was given to Yekaterina's sister to look after and would not see his father again until 1922. Family commitments were not allowed to deter the professional revolutionary from his duty to the cause.

Party Worker

The split in 1903 left the party newspaper, *Iskra*, in Menshevik hands, but as the tide of unrest in Russia rose higher Lenin was joined by a number of intellectuals who found his militancy appealing. Throughout 1904 he devoted himself to founding his own newspaper, which he called *Vpered* (*Forward*) and which began to appear in December of that year, and to rebuilding his own organization, not as a faction of the party but as the party itself. He set out to recapture the party title from the Mensheviks, and in 1906 created a secret Bolshevik Centre that would operate purely in his interests, regardless of any new arrangements with the Mensheviks or other parts of the party.

The obscurity about Stalin's early years created by Soviet propaganda dissipates to a great extent after 1905. Contemporary factual accounts show that by December 1905 he was sufficiently important locally to be invited to a Bolshevik Conference at Tammerfors, Finland, under the name K. Ivanovich. Apart from his exile to eastern Siberia, this was the first time Koba had left the Caucasus and it was an important occasion. He visited the Russian capital, St Petersburg, spoke in debates and chatted with other delegates and, most importantly, he met Lenin for the first time.

Significantly, he found Lenin's informal manner disconcerting, as he expected a 'great man' to behave towards his followers with a certain ritual; for instance, to arrive late while the assembly waited with bated breath: 'Then, just before the great man enters, the warning goes up: "Hush! Silence! He's coming!" This rite did not seem to me superfluous because it creates an impression, inspires respect ...' This, however, was not Lenin's style. 'I will not conceal from you,' Stalin wrote, 'that at that time this seemed to me to be rather a violation of certain essential rules.'[1]

On his return home, and stimulated by his experience at Tammerfors, Koba began writing articles in the local Georgian Bolshevik press. They were in the style that would become unmistakably Stalinist: dogmatic rather than argumentative, full of religious allusions, and organized mostly as questions and answers, like the Catechism at which he had excelled only a few years before. Usually commentaries on Lenin's ideas, in particular they paraphrased Lenin's obsession with centralized control of the party. Trotsky – occupying an independent position somewhere between Bolshevism and Menshevism – produced the pithiest and most prophetic comment on Lenin's organizational idea, foreshadowing as early as 1904 the reality of Stalin's exercise of power a quarter of a century later: 'Lenin's methods lead to this: the party organization at first substitutes itself for the party as a whole; then the Central Committee substitutes itself for the organization; and finally a single "dictator" substitutes himself for the Central Committee.'[2]

In April 1906 Koba left the Caucasus again, this time for the 'real abroad'. A party congress – the Fourth – was organized in Stockholm with the aim of reuniting all the groups and factions in order to mount a final onslaught on the regime. By this time, in fact, the government had largely recovered from the unrest of 1905. The new prime minister, Peter Stolypin, achieved early notoriety with his liberal use of the gallows – 'Stolypin's Necktie' – and the political scene had altered radically, with the main opposition divided by the concession of a State Duma, or parliament, that was about to come into being.

Lenin's line on tight central control was now accepted by the party, but he was opposed when he called for the nationalization of the land to be included in the party programme. Koba was among those who argued instead that the land should be confiscated and redistributed to the peasants, declaring that, as this was what they wanted, it would strengthen the party's alliance with them. It was a policy the party would adopt in 1917.

Of greater importance at the time was the issue of party finances. As the revolutionary wave of 1905 declined and the liberals emerged as the party most committed to ballot-box politics, contributions from wealthy sympathizers on whom the revolutionaries had relied all but dried up. The mayhem of 1905, however, had created a mass of desperate men – strikers, unemployed, mutineers, deserters, escaped political prisoners and common criminals – many of them carrying stolen weapons. Some formed so-called fighting detachments to combat government repression, turning increasingly to criminal acts, such as robbing banks, in order to finance themselves. Unlike his Menshevik opponents, Lenin was not above exploiting these activities through his secret agents to fund the Bolsheviks. They were especially successful in the Caucasus, where Koba – the former seminary student – came into his own.

The party condemned these tactics, just as it condemned terrorist methods, though these too were widely practised. But at the Fourth Congress of 1906 Lenin insisted that 'expropriations' – 'exes' – of state funds were legitimate and that they should continue to be carried out under party supervision. At the Fifth Congress in May 1907 he maintained silence on this issue, but by now he had constructed his party-within-a-party and was keeping most of his business to himself.

The Bolshevik faction was guided by a secret Centre, within which a still more secret committee of three dealt with combat and financial affairs. Justifiably obsessed with security in a party that had endured repeated setbacks through police penetration, Lenin had a network of agents he could entrust with sensitive tasks who would in turn employ their own 'trusties'. By dealing with only one or two such men at a time, and in watertight compartments, he reduced the risk of exposure to a minimum. That, at least, was the principle on which he operated.

The Caucasus, with its mountain ranges and ancient traditions of banditry and guerrilla fighting, was a favoured area for smuggling money, guns and explosives into Russia. And it was Koba and his small team of trusties who performed the greatest service. He took part in political assassinations and under his supervision bank robberies generated considerable funds for Lenin's operations. It was probably in a road accident during one of these that Koba acquired the distinctive feature of a damaged arm.

The most spectacular robbery took place in June 1907 in Tiflis, when Koba's gang staged a successful attack on a coach delivering nearly 350,000 roubles in 500 rouble notes to the State Bank. Bombs were thrown, people were killed and injured. The money was smuggled abroad to Lenin's agents who had orders to exchange the notes simultaneously at banks in different cities. Unfortunately, one of Lenin's most trusted agents was also a police spy, and every courier was arrested in the act.

Although the Tiflis 'ex' went into party history as a heroic episode, Stalin's role in it was never highlighted, since it ran counter to party policy and had caused a scandal. Such actions tarred the party with the brush of criminality: this was meant to be a party of professional revolutionaries and organized workers, not a gang of bandits.

Koba returned to Baku and continued his activities among the oil workers. A booming new source of jobs, the Caucasian oil ports were a magnet to workers from all over the country. In particular, Baku was home to a wide range of ethnic groups and this, combined with the harshness of oil-field life for the workers, created an explosive mixture. Indeed, while it appeared that Stolypin had crushed the revolution throughout the empire, in Baku the Bolsheviks continued to operate as if the revolution was still to come, organizing strikes as well as terrorist acts.

Koba's reputation in Lenin's eyes rose even higher: here was a man who could not only produce money for the party, but who was also carrying on the political fight when others had laid down the sword. Also, Koba was now publishing his articles in the local Russian-language Bolshevik newspaper and ensuring that they reached Lenin abroad. Lenin was impressed, not by their intellectual content or originality, but by the zeal for the Bolshevik cause shown by their author. Koba had graduated from the provincial to the national level of politics.

An essential feature of the professional revolutionary's pedigree was his penal record. In this regard Stalin excelled. Following the first arrest and his escape at the end of 1903, he was arrested again in 1908 and after several months in prison in Baku was deported again, this time to a small settlement called Solvychegodsk in northern Russia, arriving there in February 1909. He escaped after four months.

The Baku he found on his return eighteen months after his arrest was much changed. The Bolshevik and Menshevik organizations and the trade unions all had greatly reduced numbers and the party had no money. The Bolshevik newspaper had not been in circulation since he left and he set about reviving it. His first article criticized the leadership abroad for allowing dislocation between the centre and the periphery and for letting the old links wither. It was the classic complaint of a clandestine party worker.

In fact, the leadership itself had become weak, as Lenin's intellectual entourage found reasons to desert him: often it was his dictatorial manner that drove them away, but there were also differences of principle, sometimes of an extremely abstruse kind which Koba, like most underground organizers, found tiresome. But Koba was no party rebel. He demonstrated his commitment to the Leninist approach by urging that the Central Committee should exercise greater authority.

However, in March 1910, while a general strike of the oil industry was being prepared, Koba was arrested yet again and in October sent back to complete his term in northern Russia. Life in Solvychegodsk was less harsh than Siberian exile would have been, and for Koba it was made even more endurable by a young peasant widow called Maria Kuzakova, with whom he lived and by whom he produced a son, Konstantin Kuzakov, who survived in Moscow into the 1990s.

Banned from the Caucasus and large Russian cities for five years, Koba chose to live in Vologda after his term was completed, a town that was conveniently located between Moscow and St Petersburg. As an experienced 'illegal', he thought little of police restrictions and in August 1911 soon made tracks for the capital.

His closest contact in St Petersburg was Sergei Alliluyev, a Bolshevik well known to Koba from their days in Baku. Indeed, in 1903, Koba had saved his friend's two-year-old daughter, Nadezhda, from drowning when she fell into the sea. He would see her again when she was a teenage schoolgirl in 1917; she would become his secretary after the revolution and eventually his second wife. Alliluyev's apartment was under police surveillance, however, and Koba was re-arrested within a few days and after several months in prison sent back to Vologda.

Among the Leaders

By now, Lenin had resolved to effect a final split from the Mensheviks and to reconstitute his faction as *the* party. Exasperated by successive splits and confronted by hesitation on the part of even his closest intellectual comrades, he decided that henceforth he would rely on the solid foundation of men with practical experience of the underground inside Russia and an attitude of unquestioning loyalty to himself. To this end, at a Bolshevik conference in Prague in January 1912, Lenin used his authority to have Koba co-opted – *in absentia* – on to his new Central Committee together with two other Caucasians. Lenin then formed a small Russian Bureau of the same men to manage the party's affairs inside Russia.

This was a major turning point in Stalin's life: he had been upgraded from a provincial agent to a potential equal of the most prominent figures in the movement. Lenin sent an emissary to Vologda to encourage Koba to escape. Most of the other members of the Central Committee inside Russia had been arrested and Lenin needed someone with energy to provide publicity and support for the Bolshevik election campaign for the Fourth Duma.

In February 1912 Koba escaped yet again, but after a flurry of journeys to the Caucasus and Moscow, he was re-arrested and deported in April 1912, this time to the harsher location of Narym in western Siberia. Two months later he escaped again and, travelling on the customary false passport, once again found his way back to St Petersburg. There he published articles on the election in *Pravda* and earned Lenin's approval, even though eventually the Bolsheviks won only six seats. They had vacillated over whether to take part and their late entry had damaged their chances. The Mensheviks, equally hesitant, managed to secure only seven seats.

Considering his record, it was with surprising ease that Koba had escaped from Narym. Indeed, so many escapes raised suspicions that he may actually have been working for the secret police, doubts that have been ventilated at various times ever since. Such a feature in the portrait of so diabolical a figure has obvious appeal, and might even be used to explain the purges of the 1930s. In 1925, when Kamenev and Zinoviev broke with Stalin, they warned Trotsky that, if they were to die 'accidentally', Stalin would be the killer: 'His hatred of us, especially of Kamenev,' Zinoviev explained, 'is motivated chiefly by the fact that we know too much about him.'[3]

But nothing to incriminate Stalin came out when tsarist police files were opened in March 1917, and allusions to Stalin's possible involvement with the tsarist police that were made at various times after the revolution have not been substantiated by documentary proof. Nor does this approach explain the scale of the purge, which – as we shall see below – reached into sections of society entirely remote from the alleged events.

In November 1912 Koba left Russia to attend a Bolshevik gathering convened by Lenin in Cracow in Austrian Poland. Lenin was pressing for a final split with the Mensheviks. On the other hand, the Bolshevik deputies in the Duma and in *Pravda*, which Koba was now editing, wanted to avoid a public display of party disunity. This important difference with his leader placed Koba in a dilemma: he thought the Bolsheviks were too weak to follow Lenin's line. His practical experience of party organization inside Russia also inclined him towards unity, rather than division. His discomfort was expressed in the letter to Kamenev, a comrade since Tiflis in 1904, cited in the opening lines of this book.

This important issue of tactics aside, Lenin found in his Georgian disciple a fascinating type of party worker he could rely on: intelligent, alert, with a record of audacious behaviour and knowledgeable about the life of national minorities in the ethnic salad bowl of the Caucasus.

The 'national question' had bedevilled Russian social democracy since the beginning of the century. It had led to a break with the Jewish and Polish Social Democrats, and one after another the revolutionary parties of the empire's minorities were confronting the issue. The question they posed was two-fold: should the party be organized on ethnic lines and how would a future socialist state guarantee the workers' national as well as class interests?

In principle, Marxists were disinterested in this question: 'the proletariat knows no fatherland'. In practice, however, they conceded that nations must have the right of self-determination – though they would not campaign for it – whether or not this implied the break-up

of multinational empires. Difficulty arose where there
were groups that did not have an 'organic' affinity with
a particular territory, or where the local population was
mixed. In the Russian empire this meant the Jews, but
also most of the borderlands where migration had created complex communities, such as in Poland, southern
Russia – today's Ukraine – the Baltic provinces and the
Caucasus. Local movements were advocating national–
cultural autonomy, that is, freedom for national groups
to retain their cultural institutions and traditions in religion, education and all forms of self-expression. The
Mensheviks had moderated their position and espoused
the cultural autonomy for which the Jewish Social
Democrats had long campaigned.

Koba was sensitive to this issue. In 1907, in his report
on the London Congress, published in Baku, he had
pointed out that the majority of the Menshevik delegates had been Jews, followed by Georgians and then
Russians, while the majority of Bolsheviks had been
Russians, followed by Jews and then Georgians. He
noted that one of the Bolsheviks had remarked – pre-
sumably in jest – that the Mensheviks were a Jewish
faction and the Bolsheviks a genuine Russian faction,
and that 'it wouldn't be a bad idea for us Bolsheviks to
arrange a pogrom in the party'.[4] In January 1913 the
Georgian Dzhugashvili began writing under a new
pseudonym, 'Stalin' (man of steel), a name that was not
only Russian in origin but in form an obvious emula-
tion of 'Lenin'. He was now not merely an editor of the

party newspaper, but was consorting with intellectuals and even the Leader himself. He was still Koba to his comrades, but he felt it was time for him to shed his provincial and ethnic identity as a writer. Lenin proposed that he should write an article on the national question, and in mid-January 1913 sent him to Vienna on party business and to do some local research. The cosmopolitan European capital would, it was supposed, provide the proper atmosphere.

In Vienna, Stalin met Trotsky who, after Lenin's death in 1924, would personify everything Stalin came to see as resistance to his rise to ultimate power. In 1913 Lenin and Trotsky were engaged in a savage slanging match, augmented by Stalin in *Pravda*. But on personality grounds alone Stalin and Trotsky were never likely to take to each other. Stalin was still the taciturn provincial, not yet fully fluent in Russian, with a limited knowledge of the German he had studied in prison and largely ignorant of European culture. He was shabby and unimpressive in appearance: short, pockmarked from a smallpox epidemic in 1887, with eyes universally described as yellow and glinting like a tiger's. He was not comfortable in the relatively sophisticated milieu of émigré life.

Trotsky was a complete contrast. Born Lev Bronstein in 1879, he too came from an uncultured background, but he was a natural-born intellectual who, in his teens, escaped both the countryside and his Jewish roots to move among the revolutionary intelligentsia. By the age of twenty-three he was regarded as an independent-minded figure who could hold his own among the established party leadership. No less important than his remarkable intellect, he had a striking personality. Tall and handsome, dramatic in style with his glittering pince-nez, a brilliant speaker in Russian and German and on good terms with some of the leading personalities in Viennese political life, he was the consummate cosmopolitan. He was also arrogant, truculent and above all contemptuous of the men – like Stalin – who were doing Lenin's bidding.

In contrast to his relations with Trotsky, in Vienna Stalin also met Nikolai Bukharin, a brilliant Bolshevik intellectual and a man noted for his affability. It was easy to become friends with him, and in due course the two men would also become political allies. In 1938 Stalin would have him shot as an agent of British and Japanese intelligence.

Stalin's article, 'Marxism and the National Question', was his first foray into theory and it gave him great satisfaction. Not only did it please Lenin who described it as the work of a 'wonderful Georgian', but it also gave its author a valid pass into the world of the party intelligentsia. Using his considerable knowledge of the practicalities of the national question, Stalin fleshed out Lenin's position. This was that, although nationality was inseparable from territory, national independence and self-expression were not high on the revolutionary agenda. That place was reserved for the unity of the working classes of all nations. Even if a nation's working class sought independence, it would only be a transitional phase leading to their eventual unification with the workers of the world in the world revolution.

By mid-February 1913 Stalin was back in St Petersburg where he continued as an editor of *Pravda*, as a party contact with the Bolshevik deputies in the Duma, and as a militant advocate of the Leninist cause. He had especially close relations with Roman Malinovsky, the spokesman of the Bolshevik faction in the Duma. Malinovsky had been a powerful workers' leader in Moscow with the gift of revolutionary rhetoric, and in 1912 Lenin was sufficiently impressed at their very first meeting to put him on the Central Committee. What neither Lenin nor Stalin knew was that Malinovsky had been a police spy since 1909 and that the Okhrana had been instrumental in clearing his path to become a Duma deputy.

The revolutionary parties had been penetrated by police spies and *agents provocateurs* from their beginning. Malinovsky's task was to ensure that the Social Democratic factions remained divided by maintaining a hard line in the Duma. Rumours about his true role were spreading, however, but Lenin believed that his enemies were merely trying to discredit the Bolsheviks. He had staked his Duma tactics on Malinovsky and would hear nothing said against him.

Malinovsky, however, had his own agenda, and on 8/21 March 1913 he organized Stalin's arrest. With his record Stalin could expect no mercy. He was sentenced to four years in the region of Turukhansk in central

Siberia on the Arctic Circle, arriving there in August. Such a harsh sentence may be taken as evidence that he was not, after all, a police agent.

Even Stalin's will to escape was broken by the sheer bleakness of the place and the heightened surveillance that was applied with the outbreak of war in 1914. Despite the fact that by the summer of 1915 there were eighteen other Bolsheviks to share his miseries with, he spent many days lying on his bunk with his face to the wall. He served almost his full term in various settlements, returning to civilization only in March 1917 after the fall of Tsar Nicholas. Much later he would establish one of the many slave-camp complexes of his Gulag here.

Power

War

Revolutionary activity in Russia dwindled when war broke out in August 1914. Travel abroad became more difficult, especially for Social Democrats, the only party in the Duma to vote against war credits. Lenin argued publicly that a Russian defeat would promote revolution, and this led to the trial and exile of the Duma deputies. It also caused discord among his followers, many of whom were doubtful that such a seditious message would be welcome to workers, let alone soldiers.

Stalin's position was ambiguous. He remained a friend of Kamenev, who had taken the least militantly Leninist line among the deputies, but who also maintained relations with the protagonists. Communication between the exiles in Siberia and their friends at large was greatly diminished and correspondence, though it continued, slowed to a trickle. Lenin even forgot Stalin's original name.

In the few letters that Stalin wrote during his final exile he complained that he had 'never had to endure such appalling conditions'. He asked his friends in Cracow to send his publication fees urgently: 'I need money desperately. Things wouldn't be so bad if I weren't ill. But this damned illness costs money and is driving me to distraction.' In April 1914 he wrote in friendly terms to Malinovsky, praising his performance in the Duma and the press and again begging for his fees, 'as I now have a suspicious cough (with 37 degrees of frost outside), and no supplies of bread, sugar, meat or paraffin (everything gone on clothes and boots)'.

By November 1915, however, he could write to the wife of Sergei Alliluyev in a lighter tone. Thanking her for a parcel, he urged her not to spend her money on him, but rather to send him postcards with views of more colourful scenes of nature than the gloomy place he was stuck in, where 'three weeks ago we had 45 degrees of frost'. He had not forgotten her daughter, Nadezhda, for he also sent greetings 'to the girls'.[1]

Towards the end of 1916 Stalin was required to report to the military authorities in Krasnoyarsk for an army medical examination. At the end of the six-weeks journey over the frozen tundra, he was declared unfit, saved by the damaged arm. The Caucasian robberies had 'paid off' in more ways than one.

The February Revolution

In February 1917 Stalin was permitted to join Kamenev in Achinsk. Soon they received news that the Tsar had abdicated and that a Provisional Government had been formed in Petrograd (as St Petersburg was renamed in August 1914). The exiles were ecstatic. People felt that the end of tsarism meant the end of the war. Prisons were opened, police stations set on fire, destroying many secret police files on collaborators, and there was nothing to stop the exiles from going home.

Stalin and Kamenev made their way back to the capital, arriving on 12/25 March – among the first of returning exiles. Lenin, still in Switzerland, had rejected the new government as a sham and exhorted the revolutionaries not to collaborate. *Pravda* was being edited by two staunch Leninists, Vyacheslav Molotov and Alexander Shlyapnikov. As members of the Central Committee, Stalin and Kamenev were the senior Bolsheviks in the capital and quickly took over the party newspaper.

The message they published was that socialist revolution was still distant, the army must defend the country, and the Bolsheviks must join the newly created soviets (councils) of workers' and soldiers' deputies in supporting the Provisional Government 'in so far as it fights reaction or counter-revolution'. Stalin soon became a member of the Executive Committee of the Petrograd

Soviet, but he made little impression and was later recalled as a 'grey blur'.

Lenin was furious when he read the new line. He hastened back to Petrograd on the 'sealed train', arriving on 3/16 April, and at once set about bringing Stalin and the party back into line. Within a month Lenin convinced his followers to accept his policy, his *April Theses*. Where they had wanted united action with the other socialist parties, he called for clear separation. Instead of the soviets monitoring the new regime, they must seize power by winning the support of the most deprived sections of the population and, most important, by creating underground cells in the army that would foment a mentality of revolt, fraternization and desertion.

By the time Lenin returned, Stalin and other Bolsheviks had seen that the soviets were in fact a revolutionary institution and far from conciliatory. Although they were dominated by Mensheviks and Socialist Revolutionaries, the soviets had established soldiers' committees at the front and brought about demoralization of the officer corps, and through mass meetings and strikes they – particularly the Petrograd Soviet – posed a threat to the new regime.

The official line on Stalin, once he was firmly in power, was that he had played a role in 1917 second only to that of Lenin. This was not true. That part was played by Trotsky, who returned from exile in May and within a month was a star in great demand. He saw that the public mood was becoming more desperate as the promises of the February/March revolution were not realized: the abolition of the monarchy was not followed by peace, nor by the redistribution of land to the peasants. And he saw that it was Lenin who best grasped this fact, that soldiers deserting the front were gathering around Lenin as their protector, and that of all the revolutionary leaders it was Lenin who was mentally most prepared to take advantage of the growing crisis. By mid-summer Bolshevik party membership tripled to 240,000.

Trotsky had held back from calling himself a Leninist out of vanity, but he was by nature a Bolshevik, an activist, and did not want to be left standing. Moreover, like Lenin he was in favour of seizing power, and he too believed that socialist revolution would ensue if the war was turned into civil war. By July he was ready to join Lenin and in August entered the Bolshevik party with about 4,000 like-minded followers – many of them intellectuals – at the Sixth Party Congress.

Stalin's eventual emergence as Lenin's successor after 1917, however, was neither as unnatural as his critics claimed, nor as inevitable as the official biographers were compelled to write. He became a prominent figure among the Bolsheviks during the revolution. A member of the Executive Committee of the Petrograd Soviet since March, he went along with its conciliatory line until Lenin returned and uttered his *April Theses*. Stalin now found his true orientation and became the trusted executor of his master's will. He was re-elected on to the Central Committee by the third largest number of votes after Lenin and Zinoviev, and was made a member of the Bureau of the Central Committee with only three others, Lenin, Zinoviev and Kamenev.

The Bureau was the embryo of the Politburo that would be the pinnacle of power throughout the Soviet period. Now a trusted and battle-hardened member of the party élite, albeit with little reputation as a theorist, Stalin had reached the summit.

In mid-July Lenin hesitantly decided to test the government's strength by staging an armed demonstration. Although it was led by Bolsheviks, Lenin did not think his chances were strong enough to give an open lead. The aimless demonstration continued for five days with spasms of violence, and then on 8/21 July came news of a major Russian defeat at the front. As defeatists, the Bolsheviks were now seen as traitors to the Russian cause and Lenin and his entourage were branded German agents. The demonstration came to an end with a show of government force.

Prime Minister Alexander Kerensky now decided it was time to suppress Lenin. The government had evidence that Lenin was receiving large sums of money from the Germans to fund his propaganda campaigns. The news that he was about to be arrested as a German agent leaked out, however, and – with Stalin's help – he managed to escape to a fisherman's hut in neighbouring Finland where he lay low. Trotsky was arrested and the party met for its Sixth Congress without its leader. Stalin met Lenin in Finland on the eve of the Congress and it was a sign of his authority in the party that he gave the three key speeches that would have been made by Lenin.

At this time Stalin moved into the Alliluyevs' apartment. His friendship with the family deepened. Now thirty-nine years old, he brought into the family circle the aura of his heroic revolutionary past, his personal tragedies, and his evident authority in the party. Nadezhda, at the impressionable age of seventeen, had a strong attachment to her own Georgian roots, having been born and partly brought up there by her Georgian mother, and this Georgian guest fascinated her. As for his feelings, it is easy to guess that the attentions of fresh, innocent Nadezhda were a balm to his cold heart.

Events took a new turn after the party Congress. The troops of the enormous Petrograd garrison were resisting transfer to the front, while at the front itself desertion was increasing, as the soldiers became weary, eager to end the war they had thought finished when the tsar abdicated. Circulating their newspaper, *Trench Pravda*, the Bolsheviks were active among the frontline troops. Unable to give orders without first having them vetted for their revolutionary correctness by soldiers' committees, officers became demoralized. The Supreme Commander-in-Chief, General Kornilov, lost patience with his government and felt it his duty to restore order and fighting spirit.

Kornilov identified the Petrograd Soviet as the source of the sedition and asked Kerensky to let him move against it. However, Kerensky was not sure that if he allowed Kornilov to bring his troops into the capital on such a mission, the general might not stage a coup against him. Formally a Socialist Revolutionary, Kerensky was open to a charge of complicity, even though his political orientation was by now hard to discern. Instead, he armed the Soviet and gave contradictory orders to Kornilov, whose movement promptly fizzled out in confusion. This meant that the government was now without effective armed support, the Soviet was armed, and as a result Lenin was correct to identify the moment as ripe for a seizure of power.

Trotsky and the other Bolshevik leaders who had been arrested were released, and Stalin's role became once again less visible. Willingly leaving the public forum to his more crowd-friendly comrades, between March and October he published more than sixty articles and comments in the Bolshevik press. Plain in style, his writings were designed to be understood by simple workers and soldiers.

As the party's representative of the national minorities Stalin could develop his contacts in the Caucasus and other regions. As a member of the Central Committee, the Bureau and the Petrograd Soviet, he found that he possessed a natural bent for the party's backroom organizational tasks, and as a result he did not become a public figure, like Trotsky and many others. But, combining all his functions, his contribution to the Bolshevik cause was significant.

October

With Lenin in Finland and Trotsky directing the party's Military-Revolutionary Committee, which deployed 40,000 Red Guards in the capital, Stalin was a vital link between the leader and his headquarters in the capital. On 10/23 October Lenin judged that the time had come to make a bid for power and he returned to Petrograd, where he urged the Central Committee to prepare at once for an armed uprising. Kamenev and Zinoviev counselled caution, urging Lenin to wait for the outcome of elections to a Constituent Assembly, planned to take place soon. Stalin voted with the majority and on 16/29 October the decision was taken to carry out the insurrection.

The coup itself took place on the night of 25 October/7 November and at Trotsky's insistence was timed to coincide with the opening of the Second Congress of Soviets, thus creating the impression that its aim was to give power to the soviets, rather than to the Bolshevik Party.

Stalin's low profile, especially compared to Trotsky's, had been crucial to Lenin's survival, but it would do little for his revolutionary image, which he would devote great energy to reshaping in due course.

Party Manager

Coming to power, the Bolsheviks took on the full range of problems and tasks that had overwhelmed both the well-practised tsarist regime and the well-intentioned Provisional Government. They had seized power in the name of the soviets and soon soviets were springing up everywhere in a virtually spontaneous urge to begin reorganizing and managing the country's needs. Lenin therefore moved quickly to ensure that all the soviets came under Bolshevik control.

The state apparatus was taken under party management and would remain there until the end of 1991, when the Soviet period came to a close. The party itself therefore needed to be managed properly, staffed with people whose outlook was in tune with Bolshevik ideology and codes of conduct. At first, there were comparatively few Bolsheviks to take on the top jobs – none of them with any practical experience worth the name – and it was common for them to hold several posts at once.

Against this background, the seizure of power was Stalin's launch pad. Other Bolsheviks became world-wide names, such as Lenin and Trotsky, but in terms of securing a firm foundation from which to rise in the party and state structures it was Stalin who made the greatest strides. As a member of the Council of People's Commissars (Sovnarkom or cabinet of ministers) under Lenin's chairmanship, he was made

Commissar of Nationalities. A supposed expert on the national question, it was thought his knowledge would overcome the widespread hope among the borderland nations that they could take advantage of the state's current weakness and break away. It was in most cases a vain hope. The party's pious promise to respect the nations' right to self-determination was exposed as cant as early as 1918, when Lenin declared that to lose Ukraine, for instance, would be for the Soviet Republic to lose its head. At the same time, Stalin announced that the government would recognize as independent only those minority states that the party considered 'proletarian', adding that it was unlikely that a 'proletarian' regime would opt for independence from the first workers' state. Zinoviev himself, as President of the Communist International (Comintern), expressed the policy even more baldly when he told the Petrograd Soviet in 1920 that Central Asian cotton and Caucasian oil were too important to allow these regions to secede.

Stalin was also one of the seven members of the Politburo and one of the four members, with Lenin, Trotsky and party secretary Sverdlov, of an inner bureau to deal with emergencies. The first crisis was that of the new regime's very existence. In March 1918 at Brest-Litovsk, Soviet Russia made peace with Germany and withdrew from the war, as Lenin had promised it would. The cost was huge in terms of land, industry, population and gold, but

Lenin was prepared to pay it in the belief that Germany itself would not survive the war for much longer and that he would recover the outlay. Like many in the leadership, Stalin had wavered over Lenin's policy on the talks with Germany, in which Trotsky, as the first Soviet Commissar for Foreign Affairs, had come to world attention. He overcame his doubts and fell into line when Lenin threatened to resign.

As soon as the regime had extricated itself from the international war, it was immersed in a bloody civil war against a host of anti-Bolshevik armies, known collectively as the White movement. These were supported by men and supplies from no less than seventeen foreign countries, called the Intervention. Their aim was to bring Russia back into the war to protect her international interests, and to get rid of the Bolsheviks, though they shared no common idea as to who or what should replace them. This vagueness, combined with the task of fighting along a vast periphery against a united enemy who was defending the country's heartland, brought about the White defeat and the Red victory.

Stalin came into his own in the Civil War, even if in public he was overshadowed by Trotsky who as War Commissar was responsible for building the Workers' and Peasants' Red Army and maintaining its morale. Uncharacteristically for so committed an intellectual, Trotsky took the pragmatic view that to command such an untried army the regime should mobilize former tsarist officers as 'experts'. Stalin disapproved: former officers were 'class enemies' who could not be trusted. Neither Trotsky nor Lenin disagreed with this view in principle but took a more practical approach and, once the policy was in place, a political commissar, armed with a revolver, was appointed to watch over every 'bourgeois' officer.

It was during this period that Stalin accumulated the great power against which Lenin would later warn the party, and which would make him virtually unassailable as Lenin's successor when the time came. In 1918–19 he served as Military Commissar on the Southwestern Front. He had his secretary, Nadezhda Alliluyeva, with him and she soon became his 'Soviet-law wife', i.e. they lived together and registered the fact with the state. His relations with Trotsky, the supreme commander, were less than cordial and after serious clashes Stalin returned to Moscow with a sense of personal defeat.

What Stalin lost in military reputation, however, he more than made up in political achievement. As a fiercely centralist Commissar for Nationalities, who did not flinch from using physical coercion, he retrieved Soviet control over the southern and Caucasian borderlands that had declared themselves independent. Lenin commented that assimilated non-Russians, like Stalin, often became more rabidly nationalistic than the Russians themselves.

The Central Committee functioned without a permanent chairman. It was run by secretaries and a chairman was elected at each meeting. After the premature death in March 1919 of Yakov Sverdlov, the dominant secretary who had carried through Lenin's policy of bringing the soviets and local party committees under the control of the centre, it was apparent that the burgeoning complexity and functions of the Central Committee required a single co-ordinating secretary – a General Secretary.

Kamenev set the process in motion for the creation of this position. He also schemed to ensure that his friend, Stalin, should get the post. Stalin was already a member of the Politburo that decided policy and the Orgburo that deployed resources; he headed the Workers' and Peasants' Inspectorate, giving him authority over the staffing of virtually the entire state administration; he was on committees associated with the Cheka, i.e. secret police; and as a member of the Central Committee Secretariat he had a hand in all important party appointments. This combination of jobs gave him almost unique authority, linking patronage and supervision over party and state organizations throughout the country. In 1921 a British government report on Soviet Russia described Stalin as 'an organizer and a man of action … second only to Trotsky', and with 'a reputation for remarkable force of character and considerable ability'.[2]

When Kamenev's idea of a General Secretary was finally tabled in April 1922, it seemed right and proper that Stalin should be appointed. His colleagues in the leadership were mostly oblivious to the significance of the fact that the posts he held in the bureaucratic machine had already given Stalin unrivalled control of the levers of power. In that position he would not find it difficult to maintain his pre-eminence and to out-manoeuvre resistance to his further acquisition of power.

Lenin's Heir

The New Style

The Russian people quickly discovered the harshness of the new order. Born of what in 1920 Bertrand Russell called 'an impatient philosophy', the Bolshevik government would brook no compromise. The Tsar and his family had been under arrest since March 1917 and in the summer of 1918, with the Civil War already under way, they were being held in the Urals. Whether to prevent Nicholas from being made a rallying point for the White movement, or to fulfil the Bolshevik vow to rid the country of monarchy forever, Lenin ordered their murder. It duly took place on 16 July 1918 in the town of Yekaterinburg.

At the end of August 1918 an attempt was made on Lenin's life, allegedly by a Socialist Revolutionary – a near-blind, unbalanced woman who was arrested and shot within four days. Having survived two bullets in the neck and shoulder, Lenin launched a campaign of violence against all real and suspected political opponents. The Red Terror, he told his party, would emulate the violent rule of the French Revolution. As enemies of religion, the Bolsheviks were savage in their treatment of all clergy, especially of the Orthodox priests who still exercised residual moral authority over the peasantry, at least.

The peasants themselves also felt the sharp edge of Bolshevik rule. Lenin's policy of 'War Communism' was a brutal means of forcibly collecting grain and other produce from the countryside to feed the Red Army and the factory workers during the Civil War.

In May 1922 he told his Justice Commissar that Mensheviks, Socialist Revolutionaries 'and the like' should be shot, whatever activities they were engaged in, and that these activities should be linked in some way to the 'international bourgeoisie and its struggle against us …'[1] Many anti-Bolshevik revolutionaries suffered this fate, or were sent to prison or concentration camps. Relatively few were lucky enough to obtain an exit permit and leave the country.

Surrounded by hostile states, a mood of embattled paranoia developed in the Soviet government, continuing the same outlook of defensive belligerence that had characterized the Leninists before 1917. Class war under Lenin meant class destruction and its obverse, class loyalty. Stalin and his comrades were in

complete harmony with this outlook, and when he
needed a compliant force to carry out government
policy, he had no difficulty in finding it. Lenin had
decreed that the bourgeoisie would find no hiding
place in the new Russia: they would either work or
perish. Stalin developed this idea to perfection by
ensuring that every citizen was inscribed in one party
approved organization or another. These would
dole out the due allocation of food, money, living
space and any other minimal benefits the state felt it
could afford.

Two conflicting traditions had characterized Russian
social democracy, and their continued existence after
1917 helps to explain Stalin's victory over his rivals.
Dominated by intellectuals, the party leadership was
mainly preoccupied with policy and theory, and as
a consequence factions and the threat of splits were
endemic. On the other hand, among the rank and file the
norm was to accept central authority, support the leadership, avoid splits and concentrate on practical matters,
i.e. follow the 'party line'.

Throughout the 1920s the regime faced the task of
constructing the new order – 'building socialism'. No
blueprint existed and every policy was the subject of
intense debate. As General Secretary, Stalin was well
placed not only to observe shifts of opinion, but also to
bring the rank and file behind the point of view he himself favoured. And when he spoke it was always in the
name of the 'Centre', the party organization. The rank

and file would accept this as the official line, which in effect it was.

Late in 1922 Stalin precipitated a crisis in the leadership which might have blighted his ambition to succeed Lenin: he had a row with Lenin's wife, Nadezhda Krupskaya, on the telephone. Lenin was outraged and began thinking about who should succeed him. By now it was plain that, following a series of strokes, his infirmity would prevent him from returning to full participation in the management of the country. Therefore, between December 1922 and January 1923, he set down his thoughts on the personal qualities of his entourage in a letter to the party leadership which has become known as Lenin's 'Testament'.

Lenin commented on six senior Bolsheviks, each of them having positive characteristics, but none being ideal. Trotsky, though he might be 'the most able man in the present Central Committee', was also distinguished by 'his too far-reaching self-confidence and a disposition to be far too attracted by the purely administrative side of affairs'. With Stalin's personality in mind, Lenin clearly thought attitude was of prime importance. As for Stalin, 'having become General Secretary, he has concentrated enormous power in his hands, and I am not sure that he always knows how to use that power with sufficient caution'. He warned that the clash of personalities between Trotsky and Stalin might lead to a split. Of Kamenev and Zinoviev he wrote that the 'weakness' they had shown in October 1917, while 'not accidental, ought to be as little used against them as the "non-Bolshevism" of Trotsky'. Bukharin, described by Lenin as 'the most valuable theoretician of the party', and 'also ... the favourite of the whole party', was nevertheless dismissed as too 'scholastic', his 'theoretical views can only with the greatest reservations be regarded as fully Marxist'. And Pyatakov was, like Trotsky, too absorbed by administrative questions to be relied on in political matters.

Ten days later he added a postscript condemning Stalin as too rude, and urging the Congress 'to find a way to remove Stalin ... and appoint another man who in all respects differs from Stalin only in superiority, namely, more patient, more loyal, more polite, and more attentive to comrades, less capricious, etc'.[2]

Buried within Lenin's confused and contradictory views there may have been an unexpressed intention to persuade the Congress to appoint a collective leadership whose combined qualities would adequately replace his own: an immodest presentation of his own political skills, no doubt, and a hopelessly divisive inheritance to leave his comrades.

Trotsky was sure that Lenin wanted him as his successor, and he was stiffened in his own contempt for Stalin by Lenin's strictures. As for Lenin's criticism of his character, it was merely a device, he believed, to deflect the hostility of Trotsky's rivals.

Stalin could not possibly misinterpret Lenin's view of himself, and henceforth his hatred of Trotsky would mount to murderous heights. When Lenin died on 21 January 1924, Trotsky was convalescing in Georgia. Stalin cabled the news to him, and when Trotsky replied that he wanted to attend the funeral, Stalin's answer was, 'you won't be in time. The Politburo thinks that in your state of health you should go to Sukhumi.'[3] In fact the funeral took place a day later than Stalin had indicated and Trotsky was absent unnecessarily.

Stalin had established an important precedent that would be observed on every future occasion when the party leader died: the Politburo member in charge of the funeral arrangements would invariably become the successor. Throughout its history, the Soviet government established no formal or constitutional procedure for the succession of the party leader. Instead, whoever was given the task of arranging his funeral enacted a public ritual of inheritance. Also, in his funeral oration Stalin swore in the party's name repeated oaths to uphold Lenin's 'commandments', thus in effect proclaiming himself as their custodian. In due course, the official ideology of Marxism-Leninism would be transformed into Marxism-Leninism-Stalinism.

Debate and Dissonance

From now until 1928, Stalin used his position as General Secretary to organize support within the Central Committee Secretariat, and hence also among the delegates who were selected by the Secretariat to attend party conferences and congresses where policy was made and ratified. When Stalin's rivals criticized him, they were placed in the position of appearing to undermine party unity.

Lenin's 'Testament' was not made public, partly because Stalin's rivals were not united, but mainly because Stalin was already perceived by the party organization as a stabilizing force, loyal to party policy and not a loud advocate of revolutionary adventures abroad in the name of the world revolution.

Trotsky was the chief spokesman for that school of thought. Having created the 'theory of permanent revolution' in 1905, he now argued that the regime must focus its efforts on promoting socialist revolution abroad wherever the opportunity presented itself. Indeed, the Politburo had been secretly sending large sums of hard currency and gold to foreign communist parties with just this aim. But 'world revolution' was not a popular policy among the rank and file, let alone the population at large: they were tired of revolutionary zeal and looked forward to some material relief from years of deprivation. The belief was widespread that the regime should now devote its energies to rebuilding the economy and laying the foundations of a socialist society inside Soviet Russia.

Since the new regime came into being in 1917, reorganization of the national economy had naturally been of primary concern. When, by 1921, it was obvious that War Communism had failed, fostering discontent and even serious armed rebellion, Lenin introduced the New Economic Policy (NEP). This was essentially a compromise with the peasants, allowing a market to flourish in agricultural goods and small trade with the aim of rekindling the ruined domestic economy on the one hand, and accumulating surpluses to finance an ambitious programme of industrialization on the other.

By the mid-1920s, however, the coexistence of even a limited free market with a state-owned heavy industrial sector was generating serious friction. Moreover, the strain on official ideology and the intellectual tolerance of the party reached a critical level. Lenin had uttered contradictory remarks about the NEP, not making it clear whether it was only meant to provide a breathing space or whether it would continue for a long time. In any case, the NEP became both impractical and politically unacceptable.

Stalin meanwhile had been building his own position within the leadership and, no less important, his reputation in the party in general. Continuing the popularization of Lenin's ideas that had brought him to the leader's attention originally, when Lenin died Stalin published the lectures he had given to the Higher Party School as *The Foundations of Leninism* and *Problems of Leninism*. The concise, pithy style he had learnt in the seminary a quarter of a century earlier now stood him in good stead as a theorist who could convey (Lenin's) complex ideas to ordinary workers. Other Bolshevik intellectuals had been similarly engaged, but they did not have the advantage of the party's 'imprimatur' as General Secretary. Stalin was becoming the popular voice of the late Lenin, the interpreter of his word, and as such was consolidating his place at the pinnacle of power. He was also laying the foundation of his 'cult of personality'.

Stalin also caught the mood of the party when he declared that it was indeed possible to build socialism in the Soviet Union alone, and when Trotsky and his supporters attacked him, they were accused of defeatism. The charge found a genuine echo at grassroots level. In short, Stalin was unassailable and by the end of 1927 Kamenev, Zinoviev and Trotsky, who together led the main opposition, were expelled from the Central Committee. In February 1929 Trotsky was deported from the USSR. Stalin was now unchallenged as 'the Lenin of today'.

The Great Turn

Collectivization

With the argument over whether socialism could or should be built in one country relegated – with Trotsky – beyond the pale, Stalin felt free to address the major issue of industrialization and its relationship to agriculture. There was no argument that industry was the foundation of socialist construction and, given Stalin's outlook on a hostile world, that industry was needed to create a military force strong enough to defend the 'first workers' state' against external enemies.

In practical terms, by 1927 the NEP had brought Soviet industry back to 1913 levels – especially in heavy goods – but at the cost of a crisis in agriculture. The peasants were reluctant to part with grain as long as industry had few manufactured goods to offer in exchange. Stalin decided it was time to use force, and grain was again confiscated, as it had been under War Communism. He would no longer allow the peasants to threaten the cities – and the regime – with their power to withhold food. The party had been virtually absent from the country- side since the inception of the NEP and Stalin felt he could kill two birds with one stone: to reconstruct agri- culture on a collective and more politically acceptable basis and to bring the still predominantly peasant popu- lation under party control.

Bukharin, the 'high priest of NEP' who had encour- aged the peasants to enrich themselves, tried to rally the support of Kamenev and Zinoviev, his old enemies, to oust Stalin, whom he accused of threatening to wreck the rural economy and with it the promise of rapid industrialization. But he was no match for Stalin, who saw to his expulsion from the Central Committee in November 1929.

Stalin saw the issue in stark terms. He could either proceed with an enhanced form of the NEP, encourag- ing large-scale capitalist farming that would lead to the decline of the poor and middle peasantry and increase the power of the *kulaks* (the better-off peasants), and hence frustrate the introduction of socialism in the countryside, or, he could combine small peasant hold- ings into large collective farms, where economies of scale would foster the use of tractors and modern machinery – under the control of party agencies – rapidly increas- ing the marketable surplus of grain. Having made the compromise of the NEP – and failed – it was certain that

Stalin would opt for the collective farm. A month after Bukharin's expulsion, Stalin called for the liquidation of the *kulaks*, as a class, and in January 1930 issued a decree calling for the rapid collectivization of agriculture.

Stalin chose a course that was bound to conflict with the peasants' most basic instincts. A voluntary, gradual approach had failed to detach them from the age-old dream of privately owning the land and farming it as they wished. Force would win the argument. Thus, what began as an economic policy quickly turned the countryside into a scene of despair, bloodshed and terror. There had been no proper planning and government directives were widely misinterpreted by the 200,000 urban party workers and soldiers sent to carry out the policy. Many peasants, especially the *kulaks*, believed that collectivization meant that they would have to share all their possessions, and this led to the wholesale destruction of property, cattle and implements. Others thought the government would give them everything they needed.

The word 'dekulakization' entered the language, referring to the treatment of those who resisted the policy, not all of them well-off peasants. Kulaks, or the most successful farmers, were banned from entering collectives, as it was feared they would dominate them, and many hundreds of thousands of families had their houses, tools, chattels and valuables confiscated and were deported to remote areas in the north of the country and Siberia.

Some 9 million men, women and children were torn from their homes and cast into starvation, oblivion or death. Stalin even confessed to Churchill that 10 million people had been affected: 'It was all very bad and difficult – but necessary ... Some were given land of their own ... [in the north or eastern Siberia] or farther north, but the great bulk were ... wiped out by their labourers.'[1] In fact, they were 'wiped out' by the NKVD (secret police) or armed bands of party activists.

After a brief respite in March 1930, Stalin relaunched the drive against the kulaks with renewed vigour. In 1932, the Ukraine and the Volga regions, with a total population of nearly 30 million people, were struck by famine, partly the result of a drought, but chiefly because of Stalin's harsh policy. To deal with those who, through desperation, stole grain, even just a handful, Stalin passed a law in August 1932 condemning them as 'enemies of the people' and specifying the death sentence or ten years in the camps. By the beginning of 1933 more than 50,000 people had been sentenced.

Stalin sought to impose socialism in the village by eliminating all vestiges of market production. The state alone was to be the procurer and the peasants would work only for the state. Peasants with initiative and ability would be expunged from the scene. Some 25 million farming households were replaced by a quarter of a million collective farms, and the party now controlled Russia's huge rural population as it wished to. In economic terms, however, the policy led to a sharp decline in livestock and grain production, and it was not until the late 1930s that earlier levels were retrieved.

Even so, the peasants were never reconciled to the new arrangements, and by 1932 Stalin saw the need for a concession: collective farmers were allowed to sell in designated market places the food they produced on the small amount of land, usually less than an acre, surrounding their own homes – the 'private plot'. With the incentive to produce for themselves – a kind of mini-NEP – it was thought they would have the motivation to work harder for the state sector. The farmer had to acquit himself of his obligation to the collective before working 'for himself'. The policy worked, in that the cities were fed, if poorly, and the peasant sustained himself in the belief that he had some measure of control over his work. When state provision of food was overstretched, the 'private plot' would play a disproportionately important part in feeding the population.

Industrial Society

The plan to build socialism in Russia was based on modernizing the economy, grounding it in modern industrial processes and, hence, bringing the workers into the machine age. Machinery, however, demanded education and a disciplined approach to work, regular attendance, mental concentration and skill. Some workers brought these qualifications from the pre-revolutionary era and they were greatly valued, advanced in authority and well rewarded, given that their social background was also impeccable. New recruits into the expanding workforce – peasants, soldiers, office workers, artisans, in short, the whole social mix of the new society – needed training.

At the end of the 1920s, when Stalin opted for forced collectivization, he also introduced the first Five-Year Plan, a programme of rapid industrialization that turned the industrial scene into a whirlwind – if not a Bedlam – of frantic effort, impossible output targets, physical and mental strain for managers and workers alike. The accident rate and damage to machinery and production were ruinously high, and soon a climate of fear and intimidation was artificially created by Stalin as his chosen method to bring 'order'.

Stalin's New Order

Bukharin's opposition to the collectivization – and that of Trotsky and his supporters to Stalin's policies in general – had shown Stalin that to have a free hand he must eliminate such obstacles to his plan. He lamented having let Trotsky out of his grip but the rest of the leaders, old and new, were well within his grasp.

Stalin began in 1930 by rounding up leading economists who, he claimed, were plotting the restoration of capitalism in the USSR with the help of outside forces. Show trials were staged after the defendants had been softened up by torture. In September 1930 Stalin instructed Molotov, the chairman of Sovnarkom, i.e. the prime minister and his chief confidant, to publish the testimonies of the 'wreckers' of the food supply, 'and after a week ... announce that *all* these scoundrels will be executed by firing squad'.[2] Executions and long sentences in concentration camps were designed to demonstrate that failures in industry were being caused by 'wreckers' and 'enemies of the people', rather than by the party's unrealistic policies. Ordinary people soon learned that everyone, however modest or exalted their job, was liable to be so labelled.

Growth in Russian industrial output was accomplished by zeal and political commitment, driven by propaganda campaigns and material rewards for some and the ever-present fear of punishment for all.

Private Life

Those who saw Stalin at close quarters – doctors, bodyguards, secretaries, writers and military leaders – have confirmed that his 'private life and working life were one and the same thing'.[3] He evidently made few demands for his own personal benefit in the early days after the revolution. He moved from a small apartment into modest accommodation in the Kremlin in 1918 and continued to live there, progressively in larger and grander quarters, until his death. But he preferred his dachas outside Moscow, first at Zubalovo and then Kuntsevo, where he actually died.

His taste in food and wine remained Caucasian but he was not a prodigious drinker. He smoked heavily and liked to work until the small hours. He rose late, took no exercise and films and the theatre were his only distractions from work. He had his own small cinemas in the Kremlin and at one of his dachas, and from the late 1920s would regularly watch one or two films a week late at night. He justified his passion by explaining that films were an educational tool. He may have believed this; indeed, Soviet cinema had been quickly mobilized as a propaganda arm of the regime. But it is likely that he also derived relaxation and pleasure from this pastime. Through his wife, Nadezhda, he was introduced to the theatre, which they visited regularly. Later, he became almost fanatical about the ballet, attending all the Bolshoi productions several times. He went there to watch *Swan Lake* for the twentieth or thirtieth time just before his death.

Stalin had known Nadezhda Alliluyeva since she was a two-year-old in Tiflis. She was no more than seventeen – and twenty-two years his junior – when she worked as his secretary in the People's Commissariat for Nationalities. In the summer of 1918 she accompanied him to the southern front and there they became man and wife in true revolutionary fashion: no ceremony, just a public registration of the fact.

Their early married life was happy enough. She was attractive and lively, and he still had comrades with whom they could relax on terms of genuine rather than feigned companionship. Their first child, a son Vasili, was born in 1922, and their second, a daughter Svetlana, in 1926. Stalin's son by his first marriage, Yakov, then aged fourteen, had been brought from Georgia to live with his father in 1921 but he was apparently a taciturn and difficult adolescent and did not integrate well in the family.

Not that it was a close-knit family, in any case. Stalin was totally immersed in political life and when Nadezhda berated him for neglecting her and the children his inbred roughness would emerge. Perhaps the great difference in their ages played a part, perhaps she did not like the changes she saw in him: from a Georgian revolutionary he had become a powerful and Machiavellian politician. Moreover, she sympathized with Bukharin's criticism of her husband's agrarian policy, although she drew back from joining any dissident group. She had friends, especially Bukharin's second wife, but with her husband so enmeshed in the tangle of rivalry and sudden hostilities in the party leadership, she could hardly confide in anyone.

He, meanwhile, was riding high, apparently enjoying the sexual magnetism that his power brought. He flirted with willing women at parties and his neglected, hot-blooded wife became increasingly resentful and angry. She was deeply depressed and it is possible she had even been diagnosed as seriously ill, as she was due to undergo abdominal surgery for an undisclosed condition.

On 8 November 1932, at a party celebrating the anniversary of the revolution, Stalin was rude and insulting to Nadezhda. She left in a blazing temper, locked herself in her room in the Kremlin, and shot herself with a small Walther pistol that had been a gift from her uncle. The published explanation was that she had died suddenly of appendicitis; this was to forestall doubts among their close associates about Stalin's role in the whole affair, that he had not even been in the apartment but at the dacha, which was not the case.

Following the loss of his young wife – a widower for a second time – Stalin seemed to give up any further attempt to make a family life for himself. He saw even less of his children and when friends thought they had persuaded him to marry again, for some unknown reason the wedding did not take place. He remained alone until the end of his life, apart from his housekeeper, Valentina Istomina, who looked after his domestic needs, even accompanying him on his business trips. The full nature of their relationship remains unknown. When he died she fell on his breast, in full view of the assembled Politburo members, and wailed her grief.

Stalin the Executioner

The Cleansing

The 1930s in the Soviet Union was a turbulent and significant decade. It began with the launch of a massive programme of economic transformation and ended with a pact between Stalin and Hitler, the most militant opponent of Bolshevism. From a predominantly agrarian society, the country was reshaped as an industrial society in which the masses laboured with the heroic force of unprecedented endeavour and faith in the future, even if it was expressed as the Stalin cult. And from a fractious and outspoken association the Communist Party became an intimidated, obedient and unquestioning flock of bureaucrats and worshippers of the Leader.

However, the single most powerful element in this process was undoubtedly the vast 'purge' of party and society that took place in the middle years of the decade – generally known as 'the purges'.

Beginning in 1929, Stalin began to clear the way towards creating a new image for himself. The greater his claim on Lenin's inheritance, the less the danger from the opposition. The history of the party was rewritten to show Stalin in a more suitable light: as a prominent hero of 1917 and the Civil War, and as Lenin's most diligent interpreter. In the process, names that had been well known in the party simply vanished from the page, while the views of others were travestied. Official lying on an unprecedented scale – 'the Big Lie' – supplanted earlier efforts to write history from a Marxist-Leninist viewpoint, however unbalanced that may also have been.

Stalin's image was magnified to godlike stature. He was father, teacher, guide and above all infallible Leader, not merely of the Soviet peoples but of the workers of the world. His comrades – more properly his vassals – vied with each other to find yet more sycophantic compliments, as they quaked before his mounting power. His anger in private was menacing, his eyes were said to glow yellow like a tiger's.

Unlike his parallels in dictatorship in Italy, Spain and Germany, or even Lenin his mentor, Stalin did not rant when addressing large assemblies but, exploiting the microphone, spoke softly, conversationally, even intimately, eschewing high-pitched climaxes. Neither gesticulating nor jutting his chin, his movements were slow and understated, his expression either benign or sly. He derived sadistic pleasure from the game of cat and mouse. At a large election meeting in the Bolshoi Theatre in 1937, for instance, he thanked the party leaders for 'dragging' him to the meeting and 'forcing' him to say a few words. Commending the candidates – all top party figures – to their constituents, he said they might be very good Communists. Pausing for the applause to die down, he then added that they might, of course, turn out to be enemies of the people. Such twists of the knife made nervous wrecks of the leadership.[1]

If party intellectuals were suspicious of Stalin and his motives, the rank and file, which was hugely expanded after the death of Lenin with people more to Stalin's taste, readily saw all opposition as an obstacle to progress, even as 'enemies of the people'. As for the masses, they were misinformed, manipulated, cajoled and prodded into a state of unfeigned adulation for the Leader.

Yet Stalin did not feel secure. Paranoid by nature, he sensed that his critics, though cowed, were still a threat. Two years after his wife's suicide, he was faced with plain evidence of his unpopularity as party leader. At the Seventeenth Party Congress in February 1934 he reported the huge advances that had been made in all fields. His penitent former critics were now singing his praises: for Bukharin he was 'the personal embodiment of the mind and will of the party … its theoretical and practical leader'; for Tomsky 'the brightest of Lenin's pupils'; Kamenev said, 'this era … will go down in history … as the Stalin era, just as the preceding era went

down in history as the Lenin era …'; Khrushchev and
Zhdanov called him 'a leader of genius'; Comintern
leaders addressed him as the leader of the world proletariat.[2] Stalin himself uttered the even bigger fiction,
namely, that the foundations of socialism had been built.
This for him was a 'Congress of Victors'.

As the meeting glided smoothly towards its scripted
close, however, Stalin received a shock: he was informed
by Kirov that some older party members had asked him
to stand against Stalin for the post of General Secretary,
but that he would not. Then, when the anonymous
election of a new Central Committee took place,
nearly 300 delegates voted against Stalin and only three
against Kirov. Stalin was contemptuous of these 'dou-
ble-dealers', who eulogized him to his face but were
frightened to oppose him openly and schemed behind
his back. He ordered his henchmen to alter the figures
for appearance's sake to three against him and four
against Kirov. He was bound to win anyway as there
were 1,225 delegates, but he now knew that Kirov was
a rival and that there was still hostility towards him in
the highest reaches of the party. Kirov was assassinated
on 1 December 1934 in Leningrad, almost certainly on
Stalin's orders.

Stalin understood that since 1917 large numbers of
people – not only former revolutionaries – had acquired
standing and self-confidence, and had accumulated
experience and responsibility in all spheres. They were
the mainsprings of the system. Many owed allegiance to

Stalin but others were uncomfortable with his style and policies. The surreptitious show of independence at the congress was, for Stalin, the tip of the iceberg.

On the day Kirov was assassinated Stalin rushed out a new (unsigned) decree ordering the authorities to carry out the death sentence on anyone accused of a terrorist act as soon as the sentence was pronounced. The powers of the NKVD were greatly enlarged. Arrests and executions, already a common feature of daily life, now extended to the party bureaucracy, the military and the intelligentsia, as well as ordinary workers and peasants.

There was a brief hiatus in late 1936 when Stalin introduced a new Constitution, proclaiming that the USSR was a democratic state and that its citizens enjoyed full civil rights. In fact, every kind of initiative depended on party approval, and party authority was embedded in every facet of Soviet life. The law courts were party controlled and political trials were a travesty, evidence fabricated as much by the tortured defendant as by the cynical NKVD, and conspiracies were created to give substance to this parody of justice. The NKVD itself, from its head down, was purged as vigorously as the bodies it purged.

Of the 1,225 delegates at the 'Congress of Victors', 1,108 were arrested, most of them were executed by the NKVD or died in the camps, and of 139 Central Committee members 98 were shot. In August 1936, Zinoviev, Kamenev and a large group of other 'Old Bolsheviks' were tried and shot, and their wives and children also either shot or exiled. In May 1937 eight marshals were arrested, tried and shot, including Stalin's *bête noire* of the Civil War, the military genius Tukhachevsky. By the time the army purge was over, 39,761 officers had been arrested, nearly 15,000 shot and the rest sent to camps. Stalin had purged the entire officer corps and senior administrative structure of the forces, replacing them with comparatively uneducated men who now found themselves in positions far above their abilities. Most of the remaining Old Bolsheviks, along with Bukharin, were finished off in 1938.

The chief – and conveniently absent – defendant in the Moscow trials was Trotsky. He was accused of masterminding a vast conspiracy that had taken over every facet of state and party life. A wink from him, Trotsky himself wrote sarcastically, 'was enough for veterans of the revolution to become Hitler's and the Mikado's agents. On Trotsky's "instructions" … the leaders of industry, agriculture and transport were destroying the nation's productive resources and shattering its civilization … But here a difficulty arises … If my underlings have occupied all the crucial positions in the apparatus, how is it that Stalin is in the Kremlin and that I am in exile?'[3]

Trotsky's writings in exile were all delivered to Stalin by his agents, often even before their publication, and such darts found their target. Since 1930 a special NKVD assassination squad had been hunting Trotsky, and now Stalin ordered them to redouble their efforts. They finally succeeded in Mexico in May 1940, when Trotsky was assassinated with an ice pick in the brain.

Stalin's campaign of terror destroyed the top layer of the state administration and party, and terrorized the rest of society by its random unpredictability. Yet in the midst of this mayhem Stalin produced his new Constitution and declared that life had become 'merrier'. The Moscow underground railway – the Metro – opened to reveal lavishly decorated palace-like stations. Such 'bourgeois' entertainment as ballroom dancing and cabaret were permitted. Circuses were well endowed and became an important cultural institution. The film industry was mobilized to produce Hollywood-style musicals.

But the terror did not let up. The NKVD had a programme of norms: so many 'Mensheviks', so many 'Trotskyists', etc., these terms by now meaning simply any group targeted by Stalin, who personally signed the death sentences of hundreds of thousands of innocent men and women. In all, some 20 million people were arrested, 7 million shot and millions more died or languished in camp. Doom for some meant advancement for those who filled their shoes. Denunciation became the order of the day, even of outspoken parents by their well-trained children. A new class of functionaries came into being, owing their loyalty and livelihood to Stalin alone. In 1939 Stalin called a halt. His internal enemies destroyed, he now contemplated the prospect of a new, external threat.

The Nation Revived

Realignment

At the beginning of the 1930s Stalin had justified Russia's huge industrial effort by recalling that she had been beaten throughout the centuries by stronger neighbours, and that she must become strong or be beaten again. The Japanese invasion of Manchuria in 1931 stirred both Russian and American fears of Japanese expansion. The US recognized the USSR in 1933 and in the same year Stalin agreed to enter the League of Nations, which Lenin had denigrated as 'an alliance of world bandits'.

When Hitler rose to power in 1933, Stalin dismissed him as the last gasp of German capitalism soon to be consumed by the communist revolution. As the Nazi threat grew, however, and Hitler declared the USSR to be the source of a Jewish conspiracy to take over the world, Stalin's propaganda attacked Nazism as the enemy of the working class. The communist parties of Europe, organized in Comintern, were ordered to form a 'Popular Front' with all anti-Fascist parties, to moderate their revolutionary tone and start defending national interests.

Pacts and alliances were being made throughout Europe, regardless of whether their makers could fulfil them. Hitler feared a Soviet–Western rapprochement that would oppose him on two fronts. Stalin feared a Nazi–Western pact that would free Hitler to attack Russia before he had time to rebuild his purge-damaged forces. This congruence of the two dictators' needs set the scene for the Nazi–Soviet Non-aggression Pact, signed by Molotov and his German counterpart, Ribbentrop, in August 1939. The congruence extended into other areas: as Alan Bullock has written, although Nazism and Stalinism 'were irreconcilably hostile to each other … [they] had many features in common, and each presented a challenge, ideological as well as political, to the existing order in Europe'.[1] Moreover, each had world plans, detested democracy, and was skilled in manipulating lies and force as the weapons of totalitarianism; and each had his own obsession – for Hitler the Jews, for Stalin the 'class enemy'.

The Pact enabled Hitler to invade Poland and then Western Europe, while a secret protocol – whose existence was denied by the Soviet authorities until 1989 – gave Stalin a free hand to retrieve the Polish, Ukrainian and Baltic territories lost by Russia in 1918. He also attempted to annexe Finland in the winter of 1939–40, but was fought to a standstill by the tiny country. This event surprised him – and the world – and exposed the weak state of his army.

Communists and fellow travellers throughout the world recoiled from the Pact but ordinary Russians believed that their genius of a leader had saved the country by throwing Germany and the Western Powers at each others' throats.

The Great Patriotic War

On 22 June 1941, Hitler invaded the Soviet Union. Stalin was devastated, even though he knew it was inevitable. Hitler had beaten him to the draw. He had ignored warnings from his agents, and also from Churchill, and had ordered his commanders to do nothing to provoke a German attack. Newly promoted commanders, tremulous before the Leader, lacked initiative. The German *Blitzkrieg* cut through Soviet defences like a knife through butter. The Red Air Force was destroyed on the ground, giving the Germans aerial freedom to attack the retreating Red Army at will.

The scale of Stalin's miscalculation was catastrophic but it was not his nature to admit an error, let alone one of this magnitude. Instead, more than thirty senior commanders were 'tried' and shot as scapegoats, a small vanguard of the hundreds of commanders to be executed by the NKVD during the course of the war.

Soon after the invasion, Stalin created a new GHQ – the Stavka, harking back to the tsarist high command – and in August he became chairman of a new State Committee of Defence, People's Commissar for Defence and, for good measure, Supreme Commander. Marshal Zhukov, a rare example of independent-mindedness, demanded that Stalin let the generals do their jobs. Stalin, however, created muddled thinking by pressing ill-prepared offensives on his commanders.

By summer 1942, he had learned much, not only about warfare, but also about the military personality, and he had in place a group of generals whose judgement he could trust. In 1943 he became 'Marshal Stalin', regarded as a military leader of genius by the Russians, while to the West he was benign, pipe-smoking 'Uncle Joe'. In reality, Stalin applied the same coercive mentality to warfare as he had to other spheres. His orders invariably reminded commanders 'not to spare their forces and not to stop, whatever the losses'. In July 1942, in a long and angry instruction, he ordered that each army should form three to five well-armed detachments of some 200 men each, to be 'placed directly behind unreliable divisions and they must be made to shoot the panic-mongers and cowards on the spot in the event of disorderly retreat'.[2] The ferocity of the Red Army's efforts and some of its most spectacular successes, especially at Stalingrad, owed much to these murderous tactics.

In the first eighteen months of the war alone, some 3 million men were taken prisoner, or 65 per cent of the Soviet armed forces. A personal shock for Stalin came with the news in July 1941 that his elder son, Yakov Dzhugashvili, just out of military academy and at the front since June, was a prisoner of war (or POW). The Germans were making the most of this 'catch' by dropping leaflets on Soviet troops, showing Yakov in his army uniform in conversation with German officers and telling them that if their leader's own son could surrender, they might as well give up fighting.

Stalin was enraged. In his determination to liquidate anyone who might know too much about his personal life, he had dealt with his first wife's family, the Svanidzes, in the purges of 1937–8, either by shooting or the camps. Yakov's 'betrayal' prompted the execution of a remaining Svanidze uncle and a vicious decree declaring Soviet POWs outside the law and depriving their families of state support. Denied lists of Soviet prisoners by Stalin, the Red Cross was unable to alleviate their suffering. As a result, many officers committed suicide rather than surrender, thousands of POWs, including senior officers, donned German army uniform and collaborated with the enemy, and all officers and men who managed to get back to their own side, either by escape from captivity or breaking out of encirclement, were sent to special camps for 'checking'. Many remained in camp until the end of the Stalin era.

The NKVD was as active as ever. The least sign of dissent or criticism, at any level in army or civilian life, was punished by long camp sentences, if not death. Even entire ethnic groups, if suspected of disloyalty or collaboration with the enemy, were deported to the wastes of Siberia. For Stalin, discipline and control meant above all punishment and the threat of it. Paradoxically, ordinary Russians commonly responded to this harsh leadership positively, believing that it was necessary to overcome 'traditional' Russian inefficiency.

While the Allies faced the complex process of converting their economies to war production and their populations to wartime conditions, for the USSR the task was facilitated by the existence of a command economy and a society that was used to being regimented. Only the propaganda changed. Instead of Marxist slogans, the population was now exhorted to save Mother Russia.

Tsarist-style epaulettes and pre-revolutionary ranks were re-introduced, ministries replaced People's Commissariats, government officials – including diplomats – were put back into uniform, films were made glorifying historical figures, such as Alexander Nevsky who beat the Huns, and Ivan the Terrible, the first 'Tsar' and conqueror of the Mongols. Most cynically, having helped to destroy the church and the clergy under Lenin, in 1943 Stalin restored the patriarchy – non-existent since the 1920s – and reopened the churches in order to boost national feeling. Marxist ideology was played down, Comintern was formally disbanded, and militant nationalism – an essential weapon in any nation's wartime armoury – took the place of internationalism. Indeed, for the Russians the conflict was not the Second World War at all but the Great Patriotic War.

The war brought an alliance between the USSR and the Western Powers, and also introduced Stalin on to the world stage as a personality. The Caucasian brigand had long gone and now he expanded his image from Communist Party boss to world leader. In meetings with the Allies – Churchill in Moscow (1942), Churchill and Roosevelt in Tehran (1943) and Yalta (1945), and Truman, Churchill and Attlee in Potsdam (1945) – he played the diplomatic game like an old hand.

Until June 1944 the Allies were compelled by force of circumstance to refuse Stalin's demand for a second front in Europe to relieve the Red Army. In compensation, between 1 October 1941 and 30 June 1945 the Allies – mostly the US, plus the UK and Canada – delivered arms, transport, aircraft, technology and food worth some 10 billion US dollars.

Of the Western leaders, Roosevelt appeared more open towards Stalin than Churchill, who had to conceal his distaste for the Soviet despot against whose party's regime he had personally urged the Intervention in 1918. Stalin heartily reciprocated these hidden feelings. As the war progressed, relations between Stalin and the Allies remained civil but never became warm. He lost not one iota of his distrust of the West. After unprecedented feats of arms, the Red Army drove the Germans all the way from Stalingrad to central Europe and in the spring of 1945 met US and British troops in Germany. Their natural euphoric impulse to embrace and celebrate was nipped in the bud by Stalin when the NKVD reported what was happening. Contact with Westerners risked contamination with alien values. Such defensiveness at the moment of victory did not augur well for post-war relations, either with the West or between the state and the people inside Russia.

Stalin demonstrated his xenophobia and his sense of insecurity when he agreed to meet the Allied leaders at Potsdam outside Berlin in July–August 1945 for their last meeting of the war. Stalin had been terrified when flying for the first and only time in his life from Moscow to Tehran in 1943, and now he insisted on going by train. The entire route of 1,200 miles was guarded by 17,000 NKVD troops and 1,500 operational troops posted along the track, while eight armoured trains with NKVD troops patrolled the line.

The People's Reward

Already a remote and godlike figure, after the war Stalin became even more reclusive. He rarely appeared at meetings and his involvement in government steadily diminished as he sank further into the gloom of his last misanthropic years. With customary zeal, Soviet propaganda depicted him as ever more benign, wise and concerned, but in reality he was becoming an almost invisible force.

If the German invasion had shaken his self-confidence, the victory of May 1945 brought him worldwide praise as a great war leader. Yet he became pathologically suspicious. His already misanthropic outlook on the world was further soured in 1946 when Winston Churchill spoke for the first time of the 'iron curtain' that now confined the peoples of Soviet-controlled Eastern Europe. The image could not have suited Stalin better: the Soviet Union was again faced by powerful enemies and it must therefore strengthen its defences. Enemies, as the Soviet people knew from bitter experience, were likely to be as active within Russia's borders as they were outside.

Commanders and others who may once have incurred Stalin's displeasure were arrested and shot. Party bosses and as many as 2,000 officials in Leningrad were arrested and many executed, as Stalin suppressed the leadership of the country's second city, the 'Hero-City', where he detected excessive self-confidence. Political prisoners of the 1930s, sent to the front in 1941 and now returning home, many of them covered with medals, were sent back to camp. For their endurance and historic victory, the Russian people were rewarded with yet harsher controls as the reconstruction of the ruined country got under way. Once again they were exhorted to postpone the dawn of a 'radiant future' by sacrificing today for the sake of the communist tomorrow.

Stalin's paranoia even embraced his closest aides, as he lashed out at his remaining stalwarts. The wife of his private secretary, who had served him faithfully for twenty-eight years, was shot and her husband soon cast aside. The wife of the head of state, Kalinin, was arrested, as was Polina Zhemchuzhina, the Jewish wife since 1921 of Molotov, the longest surviving Bolshevik, Stalin's comrade in 1917 and thereafter his most loyal henchman. A year before her arrest in 1949, Stalin told Molotov, 'You must divorce your wife!'[3] According to Molotov, husband and wife, as good Bolsheviks, duly obeyed to serve the party cause.

Zhemchuzhina's arrest was partly a prelude to Molotov's own demotion, but more sinisterly was connected to a plan that had been brewing in Stalin's mind since 1946, namely, to eradicate influential Jewish figures as a 'dangerous alien element'.

During the war, to raise support for the Soviet war effort in the large American-Jewish community, Stalin had created the Anti-Fascist Jewish Committee. It had done its work with success but now in a world of emerging new hostilities its members were branded as Jewish nationalists. Similarly, when the State of Israel was founded in 1948 Stalin expected a pro-Soviet regime to emerge, since Zionism had socialist roots and the Israeli political élite comprised mostly Russian Jews. But Israel displayed a pro-US orientation instead, and Soviet Jews were showing wild enthusiasm for the Jewish state. Stalin smelt a rat: Jewish internationalism had raised its head. A new – old – enemy needed to be dealt with. Accused of spying for Jewish organizations backed by the US, the Anti-Fascist Jewish Committee was physically wiped out.

Xenophobia was whipped up by 'Orwellian' methods. Students were ordered to scan textbooks for the names of foreign scientists, while budding academics were told to find Russian names to insert in new editions. 'Foreignness' became synonymous with Jewishness, as the campaign focused public hatred on Soviet citizens of Jewish origin, the so-called 'rootless cosmopolitans', a codeword for Jews, although Jews were not the only ones to suffer. Anti-Semitism channelled Russian nationalism into anti-Western feeling and would, Stalin hoped, keep the people in line behind the regime.

The world of culture was particularly hard hit. Writers, literary and theatre critics, film-makers, in short the entire cultural intelligentsia, was again traumatized, as individuals were vilified in the press, disappeared, were tried, exiled or shot for 'exerting alien influence'. Western books and newspapers had long been banned, now Western radio was 'jammed', and contacts, however casual, between Soviet citizens with Westerners could bring disaster.

Stalin was of course correct, in his sick way, to believe that Western ideas could infiltrate as effectively through personal contact as through any other medium, and he was equally correct in thinking that such ideas would corrode Soviet values. Exposure to the West in later periods brought about a profound change in the outlook of the intelligentsia and political élite, so that when Gorbachev opened the floodgates in 1987 and censorship withered, the scene was set for the total collapse of the system. It had depended for its survival on Stalin's mono-culture of an ideology derived from Lenin, and simply could not withstand pluralistic and heterodox influences.

Stalin's 'cult of personality' meanwhile reached fabulous proportions, as the state prepared for the Leader's seventieth birthday in December 1949. Hagiographic epithets were showered on him and his name and his image saturated the media and all available wall space. No book or article could be published that did not begin and end with a quotation, however irrelevant, from one of his speeches. He took a personal hand in writing a new national anthem to his own greater glory. His henchman, Beria, told the writer of a film which was to show Stalin making his vow at Lenin's coffin, that '*The Vow* was to be a sublime film in which Lenin is John the Baptist and Stalin the Messiah'.[4]

It is difficult to explain the contrast between Stalin's apparent rationality as a war leader, his strategic success in bringing the Soviet Union into the heart of Europe as a military and political force, on the one hand, and the destructive and deranged violence he turned against his own most devoted associates, on the other. Certainly, it is in the nature of an omnipotent dictator to imagine enemies behind every bush. In this respect, Stalin was no exception. His food was tested for poison; his lifestyle involved minimal change, restricted to his dacha or his Black Sea residence; the circle of people permitted to come into contact with him was reduced to a handful, and his public appearances were limited to May Day and 7 November on Lenin's tomb in Red Square.

His family brought him no joy, either. His daughter, Svetlana Allilyueva, married, first, a Jewish intellectual without her father's blessing, then, secondly, the son of one of Stalin's henchmen. She would defect to the West in 1967. His first son, Yakov Dzhugashvili, died ignominiously as a German POW, shot while trying to kill himself on the electrified fence. His second son, Vasili Stalin, made a brilliant but phoney career in the air force as his father's son, but turned out a scandalous, drunken womanizer who was finally removed from office even while Stalin was still alive. He died of alcoholism in 1962, aged forty-three.

The new People's Democracies of Eastern Europe were equally subjected to anti-Western 'disinfection'. Their leaders – many of them Jews – were falsely linked in show trials with the alleged US-backed Zionist conspiracy, and contact with the West was harshly controlled.

Whereas parliamentary democracy on the whole replaces its administrations and élites by constitutional and natural means, dictatorships, by contrast, are arbitrary and unpredictable. In the Soviet case, replacement by purge and violence was a well-established tradition. Even as his own days were numbered, Stalin continued to control his subordinates by manipulation, moving the political pawns on his chessboard to balance and counter-balance each other – the army, police, government and party holding each other in check. As in the great bloodletting of the 1930s, so now the security organs themselves were purged, with senior officials violently removed and replaced by others who would soon be similarly despatched by a bullet in the back of the neck.

The End

The final chapter of Stalin's life is a story of irrational hatreds, failing health, and a plan to mount a mass assault on the Soviet Jews that only his death curtailed.

The Nineteenth Party Congress of October 1952 – the first since 1939 – was preceded by the execution of thirteen of the fourteen members of the Anti-Fascist Jewish Committee. At the Congress, Stalin spoke only briefly and he seemed distracted, probably because he was contemptuous of the institution that he had turned into a puppet show. At the Central Committee which followed, however, he was more his usual vindictive self, lashing out at his next intended victims.

Meanwhile, preparations for unmasking the 'Zionist conspiracy' moved forward. The medical profession was the chosen vehicle. In Lenin's last days, Stalin had reported to the Politburo that Lenin had indicated a wish for potassium cyanide to end his misery as a paralysed imbecile. Stalin had lacked the nerve to oblige. With lesser 'patients' he was less squeamish. Now, in 1952–3, he resorted to the idea of 'assassins in white coats' in order to carry his plans forward.

Beginning in 1951 and continuing throughout 1952, the arrest of dozens of Jewish physicians from among the top ranks of the Soviet medical profession, on charges of 'poisoning people with drugs, and killing them on the operating table',[5] made it plain that a 'Jewish conspiracy' of major proportions was being planned.

As with Lenin, one may speculate that Stalin's own physical condition had affected his judgement. Apart from an unhealthy lifestyle – working into the small hours, eating late and sleeping until midday, little or no exercise – it is conceivable that a lifelong obsession with security and the use of extreme remedies had imposed a stress that was now taking its toll in the mental and physical forms of paranoia and dizzy spells. After his seventieth birthday his health declined more rapidly. He had a series of small strokes but, distrusting his doctors, he relied on herbal teas and steam baths, remedies from his youth.

Having long lost all human feeling, except perhaps for his housekeeper, Stalin's personal life was an empty shell. If he had earlier been affected by a sense of isolation, by the end of his life it had become a genuine persecution mania.

Whether or not his fears were driving his policy, Stalin ordered the trials of the 'foreign-backed terrorist group of murdering doctors'. The long night of 1937 was to be replayed, this time with the clear intention of arousing the anti-Semitic instincts of the Russian people, barely suppressed during the more idealistic days of communist internationalism, and provoking widespread attacks on the Jewish population.

The doctors were accused of plotting to murder the Soviet leadership as a means of advancing the Zionist cause. The names of all those arrested were not published in full since they included Russians, and that would have undermined the Zionist conspiracy theory: the public could not be expected to understand why such distinguished and honoured men had sold themselves to international Jewish organizations.

Well trained to go through the proper motions in support of even the least believable campaigns, Soviet citizens – from top military down to factory workers and peasants – began reporting evidence of 'medical sabotage and terrorism' by Jews at all levels. Public hostility to the Jews reached epic proportions, even though in the 1930s, countering Trotsky's charge that the purge trials were anti-Semitic in intent, Stalin had condemned anti-Semitism as 'the most dangerous vestige of cannibalism',[6] and punishable by death. To maintain the fiction that international Zionism, not the Jews, was the target, Stalin ordered honours and prizes to be issued to prominent Soviet Jews.

Stalin planned to hold a public trial of the main accused and to have them hanged in public in Red

Square, where the orchestrated 'righteous indignation' of the mobs would spread throughout the country as pogroms. To 'save' the Jewish population, he planned mass deportations under the harshest conditions to eastern Siberia, where the 'Jewish problem' – said officially not to exist in the Soviet Union – would be finally solved.

Recent Russian research of the circumstances surrounding these events suggests that Stalin in fact had a super plan: the 'final solution' of the Jewish problem was only the prelude to a cataclysmic confrontation with the West – the final clash between communism and imperialism. As Western alarm at Soviet anti-Semitism mounted, and Stalin's entourage expressed growing concern about Russia's credibility on the world stage, Stalin apparently poured scorn on their heads and seemed to be inviting war.

Surrounded by secrecy his entire life, even the circumstances of Stalin's death are blurred. Certainly his general health was bad by 1953, if not much earlier, yet in late February 1953 he attended a performance of *Swan Lake* at the Bolshoi, sitting alone and unseen at the back of his darkened box. On the night of 28 February he watched a film at the Kremlin and then drove to his dacha, where he was joined by Beria, Khrushchev, Malenkov and Bulganin. They left at 4 a.m. on 1 March and Stalin went to bed.

Normally, his security staff expected him to call for tea by about 10 a.m., but on this occasion there was no sign of life in Stalin's room until about 6 p.m., when a light went on. Still no call came for his staff to enter, and they were under his own strict orders not to do so. Finally, at 10 p.m., using the excuse that the mail had arrived, one of the guards entered Stalin's room and found him lying helplessly on the floor in a pool of urine, mumbling incoherently. He had collapsed at 6.30 p.m., as his broken watch showed.

Not until 9 a.m. on 2 March, some fourteen hours since he was found with the obvious signs of having suffered a major stroke, was a large team of doctors – all of Russian nationality – allowed to attend the Leader. Given the criminal culture pervading the Stalinist leadership, it is natural to ask whether Beria had either engineered Stalin's death or by withholding assistance allowed the Leader to die.

Stalin's daughter and son were called. Vasily staggered about, drunk and yelling that his father was being murdered. Svetlana later described her father's death as 'difficult and terrible … The death agony was horrible. He literally choked to death as we watched. At what seemed like the very last moment he suddenly opened his eyes and cast a glance over everyone in the room. It was a terrible glance, insane or perhaps angry and full of the fear of death …'[7] The doctors struggled for days to overcome the inevitable until, at 9.50 p.m. on 5 March, they announced that the patient was dead.

His mummified body was placed next to Lenin's in the Mausoleum, sharing the catafalque until 1961, when an old Bolshevik called Fanny Lazurkina told the Twenty-first Party Congress that Lenin had come to her in a dream the previous night and said he was fed up with having Stalin's body lying next to him. Stalin was removed that night.

Within a month the Jewish doctors were released and their evidence declared invalid, having been extracted by illegal means. Stalin's successors now feared Beria as the man who had most incriminating information on them, and they moved quickly to neutralize him. He was arrested in July 1953 and after prolonged interrogation, tried and summarily executed in December.

Conclusion

Stalin's Legacy

Stalin's approach to political power was conceived in terms of control and, wherever either real or imaginary resistance might be encountered, he resorted to violence and coercion.

He had continued Lenin's work of bringing the intelligentsia to heel by dragooning them into organizations, the so-called 'creative unions', and by despatching to the Gulag or executing recalcitrants, of whom there were naturally many. For modern painters, it had been a choice between emigration while Lenin was still alive or poster-art and photography, some of it innovative and significant. Writers had had to choose between accepting official commissions for work that fulfilled the party's idea of revolutionary literature, or a life of harassment, waiting for the axe to fall.

Marginalizing his political rivals by the late 1920s, and master of the party by 1930, Stalin then turned his attention to the peasants, forcing them by death and starvation to accept his concept of efficient agriculture. The workers were brought under control by the industrialization programme of the 1930s with its system of threats, punishment and graduated rewards.

He removed all threat of opposition in the party by removing its intellectual and organizational leadership, purging the upper and middle echelons of experienced members and replacing them with functionaries whose loyalty was to him alone, and who had no qualms about applying his methods. He did the same with the army, liquidating its educated top layers and putting in their place commanders, most of whom lacked a higher military education.

The society that emerged from the cauldron of the 1930s was Stalin's creation. Through 'socio-political' education, show trials and an unending string of campaigns demanding their public show of support, the people were conditioned by constant propaganda to respond to whatever outlandish slogan, against whatever new enemy, the Leader might invent. They had it drilled into them that the system under which they lived was the most democratic on earth, and that all their sacrifices would be rewarded in the future communist paradise.

Disillusioned and even further dispossessed by the failure of the post-communist regime at the end of the twentieth century, many Russians long for the past, believing that their country was more humanely and rationally organized under Stalin and his heirs than it is today. They are understandably nostalgic for the minimal provision of life's necessities that his parsimonious regime could provide: basic food supply, basic accommodation, basic health and educational provision for the many; and a privileged, if precarious, life for a select few.

If they do not hanker for the insecurity of the Stalinist past, the Gulag and the show trials, they may still be deluded by unscrupulous politicians into thinking of Stalin as the 'firm hand of leadership', whose absence they blame for Russia's present ills. Stalin's mother knew better: on her deathbed in 1937 she said she still wished he had become a priest.

Notes

Chapter 1

1. A.V. Kvashonkin et al., *Bolshevistskoe rukovodstvo: perepiska, 1912–1927* (Moscow, Rosspen, 1996), p. 16.
2. Dmitri Volkogonov, *Stalin: Triumph and Tragedy*, translated and edited by Harold Shukman (Weidenfeld & Nicolson, London, 1991), p. 155.

Chapter 2

1. Cited in Bertram D. Wolfe, *Three Who Made a Revolution* (New York, Dial Press, 1948), p. 453.
2. Leon Trotsky, *Stalin: An Appraisal of the Man and His Influence*, edited and translated by Charles Malamuth (New York, Universal Library, 1941), p. 23, citing Joseph Iremashvili.

Chapter 3

1. Stalin's report on the congress was published in the local party press and is cited in Wolfe, *Three Who Made a Revolution* (pp. 465–6).
2. Cited in Isaac Deutscher, *The Prophet Armed. Trotsky: 1879–1921* (London, Oxford University Press, 1954), p. 90.

3. Trotsky, *Stalin*, p. 417.
4. Stalin, *Collected Works*, vol. II, (Russian edition), pp. 50–1, cited in Wolfe, *Three Who Made a Revolution*, p. 468.

Chapter 4

1. Kvashonkin et al., *Bolshevistskoe rukovodstvo*, pp. 17–21; the letter to Malinovsky is cited in R.A. Medvedev, *O Staline i stalinizme* (Moscow, 1990), pp. 25–6.
2. Russia No. 1 (1921): Report (Political and Economic) of the Committee to Collect Information on Russia *(London, HMSO, 1921), p. 26.*

Chapter 5

1. David Shub, *Lenin: A Biography* (Garden City, New York, Doubleday, 1948), p. 377.
2. Ibid., pp. 381–2.
3. Dmitri Volkogonov, *Trotsky; The Eternal Revolutionary*, translated and edited by Harold Shukman (London, HarperCollins, 1996), p. 266.

Chapter 6

1. Churchill, W., *The Second World War* (London, Cassell, 1951), vol. 4, pp. 447–8.
2. Lars T. Lih et al. (eds), *Stalin's Letters to Molotov*, translated by Catherine A. Fitzpatrick (New Haven, CT and London, Yale University Press, 1995), p. 213.
3. Dmitri Volkogonov, *Stalin: Triumph and Tragedy*, p. 145.

Chapter 7

1. For this account I am indebted to Iverach Macdonald who was present as *The Times* correspondent.
2. Volkogonov, *Stalin: Triumph and Tragedy*, pp. 197–9.

3. Isaac Deutscher, *The Prophet Outcast: Trotsky, 1929–1940*
    (London, Oxford University Press, 1963, p. 412.

Chapter 8

1. Alan Bullock, *Hitler and Stalin: Parallel Lives* (London,
    HarperCollins, 1991), p. xviii.
2. Volkogonov, *Stalin: Triumph and Tragedy*, p. 460, citing Soviet
    Ministry of Defence Archives.
3. Feliks Chuev, *Molotov Remembers*, edited with introduction and
    notes by Albert Resis (Chicago, Ivan. R. Dee, 1993), p. 325.
4. Edvard Radzinsky, *Stalin* (London, Sceptre, 1996), p. 522.
5. Arkady Vaksberg, *Stalin Against the Jews*, translated by Antonia
    Bouis (New York, Knopf, 1994), p. 247.
6. Cited in Vadim. Z. Rogovin, *1937: Stalin's Year of Terror* (Oak
    Park, Missouri, Mehring Books, 1998), p. 156.
7. Cited in Roy Medvedev, *Let History Judge*, revised and
    expanded edition, edited and translated by George Shriver
    (Oxford, Oxford University Press, 1989), p. 867.

Bibliography

Bullock, Alan. *Hitler and Stalin; Parallel Lives*, London, HarperCollins, 1991

Chuev, Feliks. *Molotov Remembers* (edited with introduction and notes by Albert Resis), Chicago, Ivan. R. Dee, 1993

Churchill, W. *History of the Second World War*, London, Cassell, 1951, vol. 4

Deutscher, Isaac. *The Prophet Armed. Trotsky: 1879–1921*, London, Oxford University Press, 1954

——, *The Prophet Outcast: Trotsky, 1929–40*, London, Oxford University Press, 1963

Kvashonkin, A.V., et al. *Bolshevistskoe rukovodstvo: perepiska, 1912–1927*, Moscow, Rosspen, 1996

Lih, Lars T., et al (eds). *Stalin's Letters to Molotov* (translated by Catherine A. Fitzpatrick), New Haven, CT and London, Yale University Press, 1995

Medvedev, Roy. *Let History Judge* (revised and expanded edition, edited and translated by George Shriver), Oxford, Oxford University Press, 1989

——, O Staline i stalinizme, *Moscow, 1990*

Radzinsky, Edvard. *Stalin*, London, Sceptre, 1996

Rogovin, Vadim Z. *1937: Stalin's Year of Terror*, Oak Park, Missouri, Mehring Books, 1998

Russia No. 1 (1921): Report (Political and Economic) of the Committee to Collect Information on Russia, *London, HMSO, 1921*

Shub, David. *Lenin: A Biography*, Garden City, New York, Doubleday, 1948

Trotsky, Leon. *Stalin: An Appraisal of the Man and His Influence* (edited and translated by Charles Malamuth), New York, Grosset & Dunlap Universal Library, 1941

Vaksberg, Arkady. *Stalin Against the Jews* (translated by Antonia Bouis), New York, Vintage Books, 1994

Volkogonov, Dmitri. *The Rise and Fall of the Soviet Empire* (translated and edited by Harold Shukman), London, HarperCollins, 1998

——. *Stalin: Triumph and Tragedy* (translated and edited by Harold Shukman), London, Weidenfeld & Nicolson, 1991

——. *Trotsky; The Eternal Revolutionary* (translated and edited by Harold Shukman), London, HarperCollins, 1996

Wolfe, Bertram D. *Three Who Made a Revolution*, New York, Dial Press, 1948

The History Press — The destination for history — www.thehistorypress.co.uk